How to save billions and billions of tax dollars and thousands and thousands of innocent children, women and men's lives

How to save billions and billions of tax dollars and thousands and thousands of innocent children, women and men's lives

Edward Varnum

Library of Congress Control Number: 2012904022
ISBN: Hardcover   978-1-4691-7864-6
                 Softcover   978-1-4691-7863-9
                 Ebook   978-1-4691-7865-3

This book was printed in the United States of America.

To order additional copies of this book, contact:
Xlibris Corporation
1-888-795-4274
www.Xlibris.com
Orders@Xlibris.com
112080

Chapter 1

Now I am deeply sorry to have to say this but as the old saying goes the truth will set you free.

The vast majority of the population of the good old United States Of America is made up of IDIOTS and HYPOCRITES.

Now after reading this book you will be able to understand WHY this country is made up of a majority of idiots and hypocrites. Now you can quit being idiots and hypocrites or you can continue to be idiots and hypocrites. The choice is going to be yours to make. I will explain to you how we can save billions and billions of tax dollars and save thousands and thousands of innocent children,women and mens lives.But it is going to be up to you the American people to do it. I will now explain in great detail why and how we absolutely have to change the way in which we now handle our drug problem. Now this is a perfect example of how we now handle our drug problem.

Lets say that there is a man who has a bad headache that causes him to have excruciating pain and that there are millions of other people who have bad headaches just like him. So they all got together and decide the only way to cure their bad headaches is to bash their heads against a brick wall. Now of course this will only cause them more pain,but they keep on doing it anyway. So now I see this man bashing his head against a wall and so i ask him why are you bashing your head against a brick wall? It looks to me like it hurts you to do this. NOW HE SAYS,YES IT DOES.

OKAY So now will you tell me why you are doing this? Well its like this myself and millions of other people have decided that this is the only way to cure bad headaches. Now does it work? No we have been doing this for over a hundred years or more and it still not working.

So dont you think that after doing something for over hundred years that does not work and hurts you. That you should try something different I mean anything that you try to do different will obviously be better than doing something that has not worked in the past and obviously will not work in the future?

NO NO NO Myself and millions of other people have decided that no matter how long it will take that the only way to eventually cure our bad headaches is to continue to bash our heads against a brick wall,even if it takes A thousand years to do so.

Now you all will have to agree that you have to be and are A complete and total IDIOT to continue to do something that has not worked in the past and will have no chance of working in the future.

Now dont you think it is about time for you to wake up and realize that we now spend billions of taxpayers dollars in a futile effort to try and stop drug use? We now completely waste and throw away billions and billions of taxpayers dollars every single year for absolutely nothing. No benefits. Now it is obvious that we have to try something different. I will now give you some logical reasons why we need to legalize drugs and how to do it.

Now it is legal to buy alcohol anywhere in the United States. Therefore it is legal to become an alcoholic. But we do not approve of a person to become an alcoholic and try to educate them not to. Now don't we.

The following is what happened when we tried to prohibit the sale of alcohol from 1922 to 1933.

Now not only should this help you to realize and recognize the stupidity of when we made the sale of alcohol illegal but how completely stupid we are in trying to continue to prohibit the sale of illegal drugs..

Now every year from 1922 to 1933 not only did we not stop or prevent people from drinking alcohol and becoming alcoholics but the number of people who drank alcohol and the number of peope who became alcoholics actually increased every year from 1922 to 1933.

I know that this is a hard fact to belive but it is true. Now by 1925 there were more than 100,000 speakeases in the State of New York alone. Now for your information speakeases were underground saloons.

We created an environment that allowed criminals to flourish,by prohibiting the sale of alcohol. The same way we now allow criminals to flourish by prohibiting the sale of illegal drugs,and thousand of innocent lives were lost and we allowed thousands and thousands of criminals to make millions and milllions of dollars from boot legging. Of which means the illegal sale of alcohol.

How to save billions and billions of tax dollars and thousands
and thousands of innocent children, women and men's lives

9

Now thank GOD at the end of 1933 we quit being stupid and reinstated the legal sale of alcohol.

Now of course we save thousands of innocent lives and criminals can no longer make any money off the sale of alcohol.

Now our government makes millions of dollars by countrolling and taxing the sale of alcohol.

Now let us look at the positive benefits that we now have by making drugs illegal. There are absolutely and positively NONE.

Now not only have we not stopped the sale of illegal drugs but we have not even made a dent in stopping it. Now for every drug dealer that we put in jail there is another one waiting to take his place.

I will now prove to you beyond a shadow of doubt, how completely and totally futile our effort is in trying to prohibit the sale and use of illegal drugs.

We put drug dealers, users, and other criminals behind bars twenty four seven in jail and surround them with armed guards twenty four seven.

Now despite the fact that we have complete and total control over the prisoners that we have in jail. We still can not stop them from having access to the sale and use of illegal drugs.

Now it should be completely and totally obvious to anybody that if we can not stop the sale and use of illegal drugs by confining and putting people in jail and surrounding them with armed guards twenty-four seven. That we will have absolutely NONE and ZERO chance at all from stopping people who live freely outside the confinment of jail from selling and using illegal drugs.

There are policemen and attorneys who defend and prosecute drug related cases who will also tell you how utterly futile our attempt is in trying to stop people from selling and using illegal drugs.

Now pay attention, we can all agree that by prohibiting the sale of illegal drugs does not work now nor will it work in our future. Also that there are absolutely no benefits from prohibiting the sale of illegal drugs.

Now we will look at the negative aspects and ramifacations of prohibiting the sale and use of illegal drugs. Number one and this should upset you the most is the needless slaughter of killing thousands of innocent lives. Number two we completely and totally throw away and waste billions and billions of tax payers dollars by putting and keeping people in jail for selling and using illegal drugs.

Number three we have people who to live in constant fear for their lives in neighborhoods where street gangs and other criminals sell drugs.

Number four we stupidly allow and let street gangs and other criminals not only in this country but criminals from around the world to make millions and millions of dollars off of the sale of illegal drugs.

Number five we spend billions and billions of dollars trying to fight terrorist groups and yet we allow them to make millions and millions of dollars by selling illegal drugs. This you can all agree is stupid of us. DONT YOU THINK?

Number six we let and allow our teenagers to have easy access to selling and using drugs.

The above are the six negative aspects of having drugs illegal. We can now eliminate them by legalizing the sale of illegal drugs.

Now just because we legalize the sale of drugs does not in any way,shape,or form say that we approve of people to use drugs.Like we sell alcohol but we do not approve of people becoming alcoholics. Now do we?

Now understand this if a person is high off of using drugs the same restrictions that we now have against people who are high on drugs will still apply.

Now we do not allow or let people who are drunk on alcohol to drive,fly airplanes or do anything else if they are drunk on alcohol. Now do we? The exact same restrictions will apply to people who are high on drugs.

Now let us look at the negative aspects and ramifications of legalizing the sale of illegal drugs by the government. There is absolutely positively NONE. That is right NONE.

Now let us look at the positive aspects and ramifications of legalizing the sale of illegal drugs by our government.

Now the only ones that will legally be able to sell illegal drugs will be our federal and state governments. They will have total control over the sale of illegal drugs. It will still be absolutely illegal for anybody else to sell illegal drugs.

The reason that we need to have state governments to sell drugs is this,to make sure that hardworking taxpayers of our individual states will receive the benefits off the money that the individual states will and can make by selling drugs.

A few examples lowering property taxes,state income taxes,and state sales taxes,ETC.

Now here is a detailed list of the benefits of legalizing drugs. Now we will be able to put street gangs and other criminals who sell illegal drugs out of business and this will be how we will be able to do this.

First off we will be able to sell drugs at half the price or more than the drug dealers can.

Therefore making it unprofitable for drug dealers to sell drugs. Also in order to help make it absolutely certain that they are unable to sell drugs at any price.

We will put a bounty on their heads. Now this is how it will work. Any individual who is convicted of selling illegal drugs will automatically be fined 40,000 dollars or more and sent to jail.

Now this is a simple way of catching drug dealers. We will put a 20,000 dollar bounty on their heads. Now in this case it will not matter what age an informant is. A person could be a young teenager or what ever age,because an informat will be kept completely and totally anonymous from the drug dealer. The bottom line is anybody will be able to go to the police and tell them that joe blow is selling illegals drugs and be able to collect the 20,000 dollar bounty.

Now with the information provided by the informant the police and only the police will be involved in the catching,prosecution,and being able to convict a drug dealer. This will guarantee that any informat will be completely anonymous to a drug dealer.

Now of course the police will have to convict a drug dealer in order for any informant to be able to collect the 20,000 dollar bounty.

Now with a 40,000 dollar fine for selling illegal drugs and minus the 20,000 dollar bounty that will leave the taxpayers with a 20,000 dollar profit.Now a drug dealer will not be able to trust anybody that he sells drugs to or any of his friends and family. Again the bottom line is that we can make it absolutely unprofitable for drug dealers to sell drugs.

Our government will not sell drugs to anybody under the age of 21 years old. Now anybody under 21 years of age will no longer be able to have any access to illegal drugs. Now just think how fantastic that would be not to have to worry about our children having any access to illegal drugs. Also the government will only sell x amount of drugs that a person can use in a x amount of time. Say in two weeks or a month. A person will then have to keep going back every two weeks or a month to buy his drugs. This will stop and prevent a person from not only trying to overdose themselves on drugs but prevent them from trying to sell or give anybody under the age of 21 years old drugs. Now people who buy drug's will periodically have to take a drug test. Why? To make sure that they are the ones using drugs.

Now here are some more positive aspects and ramifications of legalizing the sale of illegal drugs by our government. Now we will be able to save thousands and thousands of innocent people lives,and people will no longer have to live in fear of street gangs and other criminals that sell drugs in their neighborhoods.

Also terrorist groups will no longer be able to make millions and millions of dollars from selling illegal drugs.

Now the yearly savings of billions and billions of taxpayers dollars will have a tremendous economic impact on our economy. We will be able to lower our personal property taxes,state income and sales taxes. Money to repair our roads and build new bridges. Also creating jobs putting people to work,cheaper health care for everybody,the list of benefits can go on and on.

Now the only intelligent way to combat and fight the use of not only illegal drugs but alcohol,gambling and prostitution is to educate our children on the complete stupidity of doing it.

Now to simply just tell our children to say no to drugs. DOES NOT WORK.

Now what we as parents,our churches synagogues,and our government need to do is this. We have to come up with a comprehensive and detailed program. That will highlight how miserable their lives can be on drugs how it can shorten their lives,and DIE from using drugs.

Now first off is parents. They have to realize that there is more to raising children than giving them more material goods than they had.

They have to take on the responsibility of teaching their children from the first time that they are able to talk and understand what you are saying to them the stupidity of using drugs. Now they need to continually do this until as they say leave the nest.

Now second off is all of the churches and synagogues have to do their jobs of taking on and accepting the responsibility of teaching our children against the use of drugs.

Now third off is our government. IT needs to also take on the responsibility of teaching our children against the use of drugs by requiring them to take a course in all of our schools both private and public from first grade to the twelfth grade against the use of drugs.

Now we can not OVER EMPHASIZE the stupidity of taking and using illegal drugs,and that the only intelligent way to fight our war against drug use is to educate our children against the use of taking drugs.

Now it is time for our whole society to step up to the plate and take on that responsibility of doing this.

Now if this does not work we will have absolutely nobody to blame except ourselves fo being too stupid to properly educate our children against the use of drugs.NOW DONT YOU THINK?

Chapter 2

Now after a hundred years or more of prohibiting prostitution we still have prostitution.

Therefore it should be obvious that prohibiting prostitution does not work now or will it work in the furture.

Now dont you think that we should legalize prostitution because we are again bashing and hurting our heads against a brick wall for absolutely nothing. NO BENEFITS.

Now the law states that it is illegal for a woman to have sex with a man for money and for a man to have sex with a woman for money. RIGHT?

Now if we tried to totally enforce this law to the letter as they say,and put every man and woman in jail who had sex for money. We would not have enough jails to put them in and would not be able to build enough jails to put all of them in. NOW WOULD WE.

Now since we cannot stop prostitution by putting people in jail for doing it. What benefits do we receive from making prostitution illegal? ABSOLUTELY POSITIVELY NONE. So now don't you think that it is completely stupid and idiotic to continue to do so.Now let"s look at the negative aspects of making prostitution illegal.

Now numerous legal commentators point out that using law enforcement resources against prostitution reduces substantially the resources available to fight serious crimes commited by criminals against people who live in our neighborhoods and places of business.

Now how well you sleep at night is going to be your decision to make. Now do you want to see police patrolling our neigborhoods and places of business to better.Deter criminals from commiting serious crimes against us,like trying to rape our woman and or trying to rob us with guns and shoot at us and kill us. Or would you feel more safe having our police out trying to arrest johns and prostitutes of which is a totally useless thing to do? The choice is yours to make.

Now prostitutes and johns spread veneral diseases like hiv that causes AIDS. Also there are thousands of prostitutes that are murdered and we allow pimps to make millions of dollars off of prostitution. We completely and totally waste millions and millions of tax payers dollars by prosecuting and putting prostitutes and johns in jail.

Now let us look at the benefits that we will receive if we legalize prostitution.

Now it should stand to reason that a lot of men who go out and rape and or rape and murder innocent woman might not be inclined to do so if they had legal access to prostitutes and we will be able to help eliminate the spread of veneral diseases like hiv that causes AIDS. We will be able to save thousands of prostitutes lives. Now pimps will no longer be able to make millions of dollars off of prostitution.

Now here are a few facts that you need to know. One in European countries where prostitution is legal they have far lower crime rates than the United States. Two right here in this country in the state of Nevada in counties where prostitution is legal. Two professors of sociology who did extensive studies on the impact of the Nevada brothels and found that those counties who have legalized prostitution are quite peaceable and have very low crimes rates. The above are amazing facts, but are true.

Now just because we legalize prostitution does not mean that we aprove of it. We sell alcohol but we dont aprove of people to become alcoholics. NOW DO WE?

The responsibility of our children not to become johns and prostitutes should and needs to be the responsibilty of parents, churches, synagogues, and our government which need to require all schools to give a course every year a child is in school against not only using drugs but of becoming johns and prostitues, along with the abuse of using alcohol and gambling.

Now I can not emphasize this enough. The only way we can win our war against the use of illegal drugs and prostitution is to educate our children against doing these things.

Now by legalizing drugs and prostitution it will simply put, force our society to step up to the plate and teach our children the stupidity of using drugs and becoming johns and prostitutes.

Now we have to make sure that the individual states are the ones who will sell drugs and run state run brothels in each state. So that the individual taxpayers of each state will be the ones who will benefit from the money made by selling drugs and running brothels.

We now spend over 100 billion dollars a year of taxpayers money in a futile effort to out law drugs and prostitution.

Now I can not emphasize this enough that by legalizing drugs and prostitution,we will not only be able to save billions and billions of taxpayers dollars every single year,but we will be able to make millions and millions of dollars every single year until we eliminate drug use,johns and prostitutues by educating our children against doing them.

Now all the monetary benefits are too numberous to mention,but to name just a few are this. We will be able to lower our state sales and income tax,properts taxes and help create new jobs. Simply put the economic benefits. WILL BE AWESOME.

Now if you belive in GOD you need to and have to realize this. The money that we will be able to save by lowering our state sales and income taxes,and personal property taxes. ETC can have a trickle down effect of which will allow church and synagogue taxpayers to donate more money to help keep their churches and synagogues going. You need to think long and hard about this. NOW DONT YOU?

Now if we do not legalize drugs and prostitution we will have absolutely no right to complain when our personal property taxes,our state and federal sales taxes and our state and federal income taxes go up.

ALSO That you as a hardworking tax payer will be saying that there is absolutely no problem in approving of spending over 100 billion dollars of your tax dollars to be totally and completely wasted every single year to keep drugs and prostitution illegal.

Now because of the sorry and poor shape that our economy is now in and they say it will take a while for it to get better. There are families that are now homeless. Also there are states that don't have enough money to pay unemployment benefits.

So now if you lose your job and can't find another one and your family ends up being homeless like others are now. You will have nobody to blame but your own stupid idiotic self. For not being able to realize the yearly huge economical benefits from legalizing drugs and prostitution. Because you will have been too stupid to demand that the government legalize drugs and prostitution.

Now there is an old saying that you need to know and do and that is, that it takes a whole village to raise a child. So don't you think that it is about time that we do that NOW?

Chapter Three

Now you have to and need to wake up and realize that it cost us taxpayers over 23,000 dollars a year to just keep a person in jail. Now we have to provide them with a free place to live in,free utilities,like heat,electricity,and water. Also free food,like three meals a day and free medical care.

Now here is what we can do to help stop people from causing physical harm to one another. We have a huge problem of people who are married to one another who have domestic fights and cause physical harm to each other. Now don't we ?

Now if a man hits his wife and is convicted he has to pay an automatic 10,000 dollar fine and if a women is convicted of hitting her husband she has to pay an automatic 10,000 dollar fine.

Now if anybody is convicted of causing physical harm to another person they will be fined 10,000 dollars for the first offense 20,000 for the second,and if need be 40,000 for the third offense.

Simply put we can make it unaffordable for a person to cause any physical harm to another person. If a person knows that it will cost him 10,000 dollars to cause physicial harm to another person,he will definitely think twice about doing so. Now don't you think? We can also stop children and teenages from going to school or anyplace else and causing physical harm to other children and or teenagers. If they are convicted of doing this the parents and or guardians will be find 10,000 dollars. Now parents and or guadians will then definitely take the time ro teach and educate their children and or teenagers not to cause any physical harm to any other children and or teenagers. Now wont they?

Now if a person is convicted of robbery or shoplifting they will have to pay an automatic 10,000 dollars fine for the first offense and a 20,000 dollar fine for the second offense etc.

Now simply put. Do you think that hardworking taxpayers should have to pay for people who do stupid things? Dont you think that it is time for people who do stupid things that they should pay in actual dollars for the stupid things that they do?

If a person is convicted of first degree murder. What do we do? We put them in jail for life where they are allowed to socialize with other criminals,and in some states they have to face a death penality.

Obviously this has not been a huge deterent for people not to kill other people.Now obviously if a person kills another person what they are saying is that they do not care about their own life.

They do not care if they have to face a death penalty and we kill them or if they have to face a life in prison.

Now if you believe in God dont you think that only God should decide if a human being lives or dies? I do not and you should not believe that a judge or jury should be able to play like tin Gods and decide if a human being lives or dies.

Now just how stupid are we? Well we take a person that has been convicted of 1st degree murder and put him in a prison with other prisoners where we give him an opportunity and means to kill other prisoners.

Now the penalty for 1st degree murder should and needs to be this. We will send you to prison for the rest of your life without any chance of parole. Now you will not be allowed to socialize or have any physical contact with other prisoners or have any physical contact with anybody from the outside world.

You will spend the rest of your life completely isolated from the rest of humanity where you will never again have the opportunity to kill or cause harm to a fellow human being.

Now they will also be able to spend the rest of their lives regretting that they killed a fellow human being. Now I think that and you ALL will have to agree that having to spend the rest of your life living in total isolation from the rest of humanity will be a far greater deterent and penality for killing a fellow human being.

Now one way we can help install family values in our society is to try and have any child be born with two parents. There are by far way too many children being born by teenage girls and other women out of wedlock.

So how do we stop this? Now pay attention we can and should impose a 10,000 dollar stupidity tax on teenage girls and woman who have children out of wedlock, and of course now that we have dna testing we csn also impose a 10,000 dollar stupidity tax on teenage boys or men who get women pregnant out of wedlock.

There is absolutely postively no excuse for having children out of wedlock being that birth control pills are available to any teenage girls or women and condoms for any teenage boys and men.

That being said parents and guardians of teenage girls and boys under the age of 18 years will be held liable for the 10.000 dollar stupidity tax. Now this will definitely discourage not only any teenage girl or boy but more importantly any parents or guardians from letting their daughter get pregnant or having their son be responsible for getting a girl pregnant.

Now simply put and the bottom line is this,don't you think that children deserve to have two parents when they are born? Also why should hardworking taxpayers have to pay public aid to stupid people who have children out of wedlock.

Now if idiot people want to have children out of wedlock fine. I say let them do it as long as they are willing to each, a women and a man want to pay a 10,000 dollar stupidity tax. Because that means there will be less taxes hardworking tax payers will have to pay.

Chapter Four

I am sick and tired of hearing people complain about how they had to grow up in poor neighborhoods, or how they now are living in poor neighborhoods.

I will now tell you what it was like when I grew up. Now I was born in 1944 and it was not until I was seven or eight years old that we had indoor plumbing. Now before we got indoor plumbing when I wanted to go to the bathroom I had to use our outhouse. Now when Halloween came around Halloween pranksters would come around and tip our outhouse over.

We had a water pump on our back porch that we had to use for drinking water and bath water. Now for heating our house we had a pot belly coal burning stove of which sat in our living room. We had a two story house of which our bedrooms were upstairs, needless to say when we went to bed in the winter time and got under our bed covers we stayed there until it was time to get up the next morning.

Now a couple of weeks before Halloween we finally got indoor plumbing so when the pranksters tipped over our out house they actually did us a favor. Now the only home entertainment we had when I was young was listening to radio programs like The Lone Ranger, The Shadow.MR and Mrs North,Etc. in the evening. I played out side with the neighbohood kids during the day.

Now when we first got a T.V set we only had three channels, ABC,NBC, and CBS. And it was black and white set.It was not until later years that they come out with color T.V and NBC was the first network to come out with color programs. Now of course we did not have remote controls, we had to get up and change channels by hand.

My family did not have a car until I graduated from school and got a job, and was able to afford to buy an inexpensive used car.Now when

I was growing up I went to school with black kids and we all got along fine no problems. When I got out of school and got a job I worked with black people. We had no racial problems. The bottom line we all treated each other the same. WHY Because we shared a common bond both white people and black people were both poor.

NOW PAY ATTENTION. People in this country put way too much emphasis on material goods and money. Now just because some people who have a lot of material goods and money they think that they are better than other people who don't have a lot of material goods and money. They think that people will like them better than people who don't have a lot of material goods and money and be their friends.

Now true friends will not judge you by how much money or material goods you have. They will judge you by how you are as an individual human being. Now myself and other people have a lot of good friends. But we would not have any friends if they judged us by how much money or material goods we have.

Now think about this. Take a good look at how many rich and famous people you hear about that become addicted to drugs and die from drug over dose or become alcoholics. Now there are some people who are rich and famous that I respect and admire. They are the ones that have their priorities straight. They take time off from their careers to spend time with their family and friends.

They realize and know that most important thing in life is spending time with their family and friends who care and judge them for who they are as an individual and not judge them by how rich or famous they are. Now think long and hard about this. NO matter how much money you have or material goods you have in your life. YOU can not take them with you when you DIE.

ALSO If you believe in GOD Do you believe that GOD will judge you by how much money and material goods you have in order to get you into heaven? OR That he will judge you by how you treated your fellow human beings in order to get into heaven.

Also back then when I was growing up we did not have a population problem. WE DO NOW. Now here is a fact that you really need to think about the world population now stands at 7 billion people.

Now pay close attention. It is imperative that we instute population control now. Not only in this country but around the world. WHY? Because if we don't do it we will be condeming our future generations to a life of starvation. Now as the old saying goes you do not have to be a rocket scientist to figure this out. The planet earth is only capable of supporting X amount of people.

Now since our country was founded over 250 years ago with a small population we have been able to increase it to over 300 million people. It should now be obvious that it will take less than a hundred years to double our population to over 600 hundred million people or a billion people. Now do you really think that this country in the near future will be able to support a billion people?

Now all you have to do is look around you and see what I see is happening in this country right now. Land to grow food on is now being used for commericial development at a rapid pace. We also are using up our fresh water supply at at a rapid pace.

Now our future generations will be lucky if they have enough water to drink let alone have enough to bathe with or to use to go to the barhroon. Wakeup people right now we are trying to come up with ways to conserve our fresh water supply. Our world population is growing as fast pace. I just used our country as an example of how fast our world population is growing. Now what can we do to control our world wide populaion explosion? The simple fact is that we now have the means to control not only our population explosion in this country but around the world.

Now we have plenty of birth control pills and condoms in this country to use so it will be easy for us to institute population control. Now we have to and need to get together with th United Nations and institute a foreign aid policy of which will consist of helping supply other countries of the world with birth control pills and condoms. But because if we do not do this now in the near future in this country alone we will not be able to produce enough food and water for our own population explosion let alone to even try to help a world wide population explosion.

Now I am 100 per cent sure that we will be too stupid to institute a population control plan in this country and around the world. WHY? Because right now we don't have a huge population problem, Simply put we are too stupid to worry about our future generations. Now I have a plan that will work to save some of our future generations from starving to death. But it will only work for you people who are smart enough to institute it now.

And who care about their grand children,great grand children,etc. Now my plan is to publish a book on how to cook a human being because that will be the only food source left for our future generations left to eat. Now if you are smart you will buy this book now and pass it on to your future generations. Now pay attention we have done what God wanted us to do. We have gone forth and multiplied.

Now do you really believe that God wants us to go forth and continue to multiply ourselves out of exsistence? I now apologize to you God for our stupidity. You gave us brains but as you can see we are too stupid to use them to control our population explosion.

Chapter Five

Now Hurrican Katrina will show you just how much of A racist attitude black people have against white people. Now before the city of New Orleans was hit with the hurrican the black mayor of New Orleans was notified by A personal phone call that stated that the city of New Orleans was going to be hit with a severe hurrican that would cause severe damage.

Now the black mayor of New Orleans after hearing this should have ordered an immediate evacuation of the city. Don't you think? BUT HE DID NOT. Why? Now because he failed to evalcate the city it turned out to be a huge mistake. NOW DIDNT IT?

Now if the mayor of New Orleans was white black people would be calling him a big white racist pig for not evacuating the city of New Orleans before the hurrican hit. RIGHT?

Now again after the hurrican hit the city the black mayor did absolutely nothing to help evacuate the black people and white people. He just sat back and waited for the federal government to do something.

Now if a white mayor would have sat back and did nothing to help evacuate the city and would have waited for the federal government to do something black people would have jumped all over him for not doing anything. RIGHT?

Now when they started to rebuild the city the black mayor stated that he wanted to chocolatize the city of New Orleans. Now if a white mayor of New Orleans would have said that he was going to vanillaize the city black people would have crucified him for making that statement. RIGHT?

Now A black person stated on national TV that the slow responce to the hurrican victims was because President Bush did not like black people. Now instead of making that racist remark he should have said that President Bush does not like poor people in this country, and he might have been right.

How to save billions and billions of tax dollars and thousands
and thousands of innocent children, women and men's lives

25

Now I know that this is going to be hard for millions of black people to believe,because poor white people are invisible and dont exist according to black people.

But there were poor white people who were in the same boat as black people and were victims of the hurrican. Now the huge problem is that black people did not even acknowledge that there were poor white people in the same boat as they were.

Now I am going to ask black people this question why do you believe that you are the only poor people who live in this country? Why do you not want to acknowlege and accept that there are POOR Mexicans,Japanese,Chinese,White People, and other Races that live in this country?

Now how racist are black people? Well for one thing they have a United Negro College Fund, and they state that a mind is a terrible thing to waste. Now don't they?

Now they are saying that they do not care if poor Mexicans,Japanese,Chinese,White or other races minds are wasted Now do they? Now can you imagine if POOR Mexicans,Japanese,Chinese,White people or other races started an individual college funds for their individual races. Black Americans would all scream to high heaven about how racist they would be. Now wouldnt they?

Now don't you think that black Americans and all other races should all get together and start a college fund for all poor human beings regardless of race.

We also have all black colleges and universities but that is too all right. As long as we do not have all Japense,Chinese or any other races colleges and universities because that would be racist, Right?

Now black people believe in reparation and I do too. Now black people believe that white people should have to pay for what white peoples and ancestors did over 200 years ago, by having black people as slaves. FINE. So now black people should come up with x amount of dollars that white people should pay black people.

Now after you do that then it will be white peoples turn to come up with x amount of dollars that black people should pay to white people. Why? For all the thousands and thousands of white peoples ancestors who died fighting in the Civil War to free black slaves.

Now simply put to all black people. Pay Attention If it was not for the millions of white peoples ancestors who did not believe in slavery all black people would still be slaves TODAY. Now think long and hard about that.

Now we have strict laws that prevent people from being racist in this country.Now it comes down to attitude and black people have the biggest racist attitude in this country.They teach and promote a racist attitude not only against other races but against their own race.

Black people say that it is totally and completely wrong to judge a person by the color of their skin Right and to call a black person a niggar. Now it is a damn shame that black people think and believe that it is all right for them to be two faced and live by a double standard BECAUSE THEY DO NOT PRACTICE WHAT THEY PREACH.

Black people believe that it is all right for them to call each other niggars and wrong for other races to call them niggars because if other races call them niggars they are considerd as being racist, and they also believe it is all right for them to judge other races by the color of their skin.

Pay attention white people and other races, there is absolutely no reason for you to call black people niggars.Because black people do a great and fantastic job of calling themselves niggars. Now black people want to openly recognize that all black people are niggars. Now that is all right for them to do that. The problem is that black people want to be known as African Americans.

Now since black people believe and approve of calling themselves niggars and being racist against other races. You have to quit calling yourselves Africans. You have absolutely no right to degrade and slander the word African.

We now live in a global society. People of other nations around the world have access to and see TV programs and hollwood films. They see African American actors and comedians calling other African Americans niggars. And making racist remarks against other races.

Now by doing so you are broadcasting a completely and totally false impression that all Africans and black people who live in other countries of the world are niggars and racist. You can not expect other people of the world to be able to make a clear and distinct difference between African black Americans and. African black people and black people who live in other countries around the world.

Now black people who live in Africa and around the world are not and I repeat NOT NIGGARS AND RACIST. Therefore you should no longer be allowed to call yourselves African Americans. Now Since you do not care and believe it is all right to call each other niggars. You should have absolutely no problem in calling yourselves American niggars. Now by calling yourselves American NIGGARS you will leave no doubt that just black Americans are niggars. And not other black people of the world.

Now it will be all right for black actors and comedians to broadcast to the rest of the world that black Americans and only black Americans are niggars and racist. Now since black people want to degrade each other there is another non racist way to do this.and that is to call all black people ASSHOLES. Because all races have people in them who are known as ASSHOLES.

Now it will be perfectly all right for all black people black actors and comedians to broadcast to the world that all black people are ASSHOLES and want to be known as Asshole Americans. Now black people say that they have this amazing ability to remember what it was like to live over 200 years ago as slaves.

Now you all have to admit that is truely amazing that out of the billions of people who live on this planet that they are the only ones who have this ability. It is a shame though that they can only remember what was like to be slaves. It is too bad that they can not remember the Emancipation Proclamation and the Civil War etc.

Now black people should want to be studied by experts to see how they have this amazing ability to live in and remember the past of over 200 years ago. Now if it is a chemical in the brain that allows them to do this. It should be duplicated because this will allow black people to make millions of dollars off of selling it. RIGHT?

WHY? Think about this.It would allow a person to go back in time to a specific time period and be able to remember what it would be like living as a slave in times past,like Egyptian and Roman times, etc.or as royalty in past times. Now dont you think that would be an awesome thing to be able to do?

Now if this ability to remember living as a slave in the past is not chemical. Then we have to assume that it is brought on by having to live next to and be surrounded by white people that triggers this effect. Therefore for the mental health and mental well being of all black people. All black people need to and should go back to their home land of Africa from which all black people come from.

There you will be able to be surrounded by your descendants of your African ancestory.Now you will be able to live without any white people around to remind you of being slaves in this country and being oppressed by white people for over 200 years in this country.

Now by living in Africa this will allow all black people to over come this huge mental problem that they all say that they have by living in this country.Also this is the only logical reason that black people are able to ignore the fact that 360 thousand union troops and other white people gave thier lives to free black people from slavery.

Now black people also want to ignore the following.

Now white people enacted laws against racism and discrimination against black people. But it is not enough to make black people happy. Black athletes make up to 80 to 90 oercent of profesional and college football and basketball teams. The pro athletes make millions of dollars and the college athletes get free scholarships.

Now the vast matority of fans who support and go and see pro and college teams play and see them play on TV are white people. But black people ignore this fact.Also we have black actors,actresses,musicians, and comedians who make millions of dollars because of white people who support them by going to see them.

We have black politicians some who are mayors of major U.S. cities,black senators and a black president because white people voted for them. Now it is mind boggling to realize that no matter how much support white people give black people it will never be enough.

Now to show you how stupid white people are check this out. Now according to black people even though we have strict laws against racism in hiring people,black Americans still claim that they can not get a job because of white people. It is still white peoples fault. Now that being said. I can not figure out why white people are too stupid to use the same system that black people say that we use against them to get jobs to. Prevent and stop illegal Mexicans who speak no English to get jobs.

I think the problem is that white people are to stupid to understand and are unable to comprehend the system black people say that we use to prevent them from getting jobs. Therefore white people have to quit being stupid and ask black people to come right out and explain in great detail the system white people now use to stop black Americans from getting jobs so white people can use this system to stop and put a halt on illegal Mexicans from getting jobs in this country. Now dont you think?

Now I have seen where black people will move into a white neighborhood and white people will move out until it becomes an all black neighborhoods. Now about ten years later black people will start complaining that they are living in a trashy rundown slum neighborhood and that it is all white peoples fault. Now in Chicago they built apartment buildings for poor black people to live in.

Now again black people will blame white people for having to live in trashy rundown apartment buildings. Now I think that I have figured out why it is white people fault for black people having to live in trashy rundown neighborhoods. The reason is and you all will have to agree is this white people sneak into black neighborhoods in the middle of the night and trash their neighborhoods.

Now white people should and need to be held accountable for black peoples living conditions. We have to immediatly pass a law that will prohibits white people from sneaking in the middle of the night into black neighborhoods and trashing and tearing down black peoples homes and apartment buildings. Now when white people are caught doing this they will automatically be fined 20,000 dollars and sent to jail for two years.

As a matter of fact we need to have a constititional amendment prohibiting this. Now pay attention white people you will no longer be allowed to sneak into black neighborhoods and trash and tear down black peoples homes and apartment buildings.

Now one way to slove this mental racial problem is for all races of people in this country to join together and force the government to spend billions of dollars to build a time machine.

With this time machine we will be able to go back in time and stop and prevent white slave owners from bringing black people into this country. We will be able to enact strict laws prohibiting any white people from bringing any black people into this country. Now any white people caught bringing black people into this country will automatilally be executed and all black people will be sent back to Africa.

Now we all know that if it was not for white slave owners we would have no black people living in this country and black people would be living a happy and care free life in Africa. Now this should be a huge incentive to motivate our government to spend the bilions of dollars needed to try and invent a time machine. Knowing that all black people will be extremely happy to be born in and live in Africa and not this country. RIGHT?

Now the only logical reason black people can say that white people living now should be held accountable for what white people did to black people over two hundred years ago is that they have found out that white people have invented a time machine and are refusing to use it to go back in time and prevent white people from bringing black people to this country from Africa.

They still think that they deserve some sort of reparations for what white people did over 200 years ago.And they continue to have a racist attitude toward white people. The big problem is that black people like to blame white people for black people who are poor. And that it is white peoples fault because all black people are not rich.

Now it is obvious that black people have not been happy living in this country in the PAST,NOW or will be in the FUTURE. Now because white people dont want to use the time machine and go back in time to stop and prevent black people from entering this country. Therefore it is going to be white people responsibility to give black people the only proper reparation that obviously that black people want.

And that is a free one way transportation trip back to Africa. Now white people have to realize this it is wrong now and has been wrong for over 200 years to force black people to live in this country. The only way black people can truly be free is for them to move back to AFRICA from which white people wrongfully brought them.

Therefore it is going to be white peoples responsibility to pay for and send all black people back to AFRICA. Where they will all be able to live happily and be able to all be rich without any white people around to stop all of them from being rich.

Now white people will have to make sure that no black people are left behind. So that all black people will be able to live happily ever after in Africa. Now black people you will have to learn to be patient because it is going to take billions of dollars to raise and at least twenty or thirty years or more to give you all free transportation back to AFRICA.

Now what we have to do in this country with great urgency is to teach and have everybody who lives in this country learn to treat and judge everybody as INDIVIDUAL HUMAN BEINGS.Reguardless of thier nationality, religion or anything else.

Now black people do not get mad. I know that you do not want to be treated as individual human beings, and do not want to treat anybody else as individual human beings. But as long as you are living in this country you will be treated simply as a human being and you will be expected to treat all other people simply as human beings.

Now remember black people this will only be a temporary thing for you to do until you all can be given free transportation back to AFRICA. Now we have to start teaching our children in both private and public schools from preschool to every year that they are in school until they graduate that the person sitting next to them is a human being and has to be treated and judged as an individual human being reguardless of their race,religion and or anything else.NOW DONT YOU THINK?

Now we love to say that in this country that all men are created equal right? What a huge joke that is. Now if all men are created equal in this country, then explain why we are required to state what race we are on certain forms that we are required to fill out.

Now this is being what you can call the ultimate in being hypocrits. Now it is a mind boggling and amazing to realize that we have no group of people living in this country who are know as or want to be know as simply Americans. We love to sterotype and label everybody in this country and be known because of our nationality or religion.

Examples are people who love to state that they are Italians,Mexicans ,Irish,Africans,Baptist,Atheists etc,etc.To me it is and it should be to you a shame that nobody wants to be know simply as an American.Now dont you agree?

Now if you truly believe that all men are created equal in this country then you will have to stop stereotyping and labeling people in this country. DONT YOU THINK? That means that we will no longer have any Mexican,Irish,African, etc,etc communities, or label anybody by there religion.

Now we will simply be know as American communities. And the people who live in these communities are all individual human beings. And have to be treated and judged as such. Now don't you think? It is time to quit sterotyping and labeling people and start treating people as individual human beings. Because that is exactly what we all are. Nothing more or less than human beings who share this planet earth that we live on will billions of other human beings.

Now after reading this you the people who live in this country will have to decide if all men are created EQUAL OR NOT. Now if you truly belive that all men are created equal you will stop stereotyping and labeling people. Now if you dont you will continue to stereotype and label people.

As the saying goes the choice is your to make. Now think about this. Do you believe that GOD stereotypes and labels people or does he judge people as individual human beings?

Chapter Six

Now we have a school system that is completely and totally INADEQUATE. Now if we want to give all of our children a better education this is what we have to do. We need to completely change our present school system. Now the first and most obvious thing that we have to do is provide our children with teachers that know how to teach. We now allow and subject our children to teachers that do not know how to teach. This is unbelievably stupid of our society to allow this to happen.

Now this should prove to you that we have teachers that don't know how to teach. They advertise on TV that you should send your kids to learning centers where they have teachers who know how to teach your kids how to learn. Now that is what you can call pathetic, and obvious that we don't have teachers in our schools system that know how to teach. IF we did have all of our teachers to know how to teach we would not need any learning centers. NOW would we?

Then again maybe we do need them. What we should do is send our teachers to the learning centers where their teachers can teach our teachers on how to teach kids how to learn.Now don't you think? Now when I went to school in the fifties and sixties we had teachers who knew how to teach.

NOW an example is that we had a geometry teacher who would go to the black board and explain in detail how to arrive at a correct solution to our geometry problems that we were doing. NOW this is what you can call teaching. EXPLAINING in detail the subject that you are teaching them. NOW my son had a math teacher who did not know how to teach.

NOW instead of going to the blackboard and teaching my son how to arrive at a proper solution to the math problems he just gave him the answers to the math problems and expected him to figure out how to come up with the correct solution instead of teaching him how to come up with correct solution to the problem.

Now I went to the school principal and complained to him that my son's math teacher did not know how to teach. That the only thing he did was give my son homework with the answers and tests. That being said he did not try to justify the math teacher as being able to teach. So I told him that apparently the only thing you need to know to be teacher is how to read and write and that I could do that and for him to give me a job as a teacher. Again no response. Now his response to my questions told me the obvious that there was nothing he could do about having a teacher who could not teach.

WHY Because we have teachers unions. AS LONG as a teacher belongs to a teachers union. WE have to PAY them whether they can teach or not. NOW that is what you can call a pathectic school system. BECAUSE the teachers union protects teachers who do not know how to teach. Now the way to stop this is simple We simply put prospective teachers on a one or two year probation period. by a review board.

Now a review board will then be able to decide whether a prospective teacher is qualifide to teach or not. Obviously if they find that a teacher is not qualified to teach they will be fired. IF they find that the prospective teacher is qualified to teach they then will be allowed to join the teachers union. NOW don't you think that our number one priority should be to make sure that we have qualified teachers to teach our children?

Now I have heard on TV that our school system ranks 20th or lower compared to other school systems in other countries of the world. NOW that is pathectic. Now I have seen on TV two TV shows that prove how inadequate our school system is. Now both shows would randomly pick three people off our streets and ask them questions that anybody with a proper high school education would be able to answer.

Now on both shows over 80 percent of the questions they asked them, They would get the answers wrong. Now this should prove beyond a shadow of doubt that we have to change our school system with qualified teachers. Now a course that needs to be a mandatory course is U.S GEOGRAPHY. WHY because I seen a teacher on WHO WANTS TO BE A MILLIONAIR. Miss a really easy U.S GEOGRAPHY question.

They asked the teacher what state was EAST ST LOUIS located in. The teacher did not know because the teacher did not know obviously that ST LOUIS MO is located next to the state of Illinois. Now that is what you can call pathetic. Now another required course we need to teach is how to cook meals. WHY? ONE IT is a lot cheaper to go to the grocery store and buy groceries to take home and cook rather than spending money at fast food restaurants.

Two and the most important thing to teach our students is how to cook healthy meals.Now pay attention obesty is a huge problem in this country. We have way too many children,teenagers, and adults that are over weight.Now you should all agree that this cooking class needs to be taught to help fight obesity.

Now there is another course that students need to take and learn and that is MONEY MANAGEMENT. Now we need to teach them to live within their means. In other words how to get by with the money that they will make in a year, whether it is 20,000 or 100,000 a year. The simple fact is that no matter how much money a person makes in a year a vast majority of people will try to live and spend more money than they make in a year. Now they need to be taught to shop around when they need an item.

Different stores charge different prices for the exact same item you are looking for. So buy it at the store that sells it the cheapest. Now all stores come out with items on sale. When they do stock up on non perishable items that you use on a regular basis.Now what we all so need to teach students and most importent is how to manage a checking and savings account. We need to teach them how to write checks and balance a checking account.

Now this is what you can call throwing away money for simply being stupid. A lot of people will pay a business X amount of dollars to cash a payroll check and other checks. Now if you have a checking account with a bank they will charge you absolutely nothing to cash your payroll check or any other checks.

Again throwing money away because you don't know how to manage a checking account is idiotic. Now last but not least how to manage a credit card. To be a loan shark is supposed to be illegal in this country. I say supposed to be because we allow credit card companies to charge what ever amount of interest rates they want to. If you get a credit card make absolutely sure that you pay it off at the end of the month.

Otherwise you will be wasting a lot of money paying a ridiculous amount of interest. Now teachers giving children home work to do at home is a completely and totally idiotic thing to do. WHY? After a child gets home from school the last thing a child wants to do is to have to spend a hour or more doing home work. Now I do not blame them for not wanting to do this. There are two important reasons whay this is a very difficult task to expect children to do.

The first reason is this.Not only is it difficult to expect children to find the time to do home work at home after school, but to expect them to find a quiet place in their home to be able to totaly concentrate on their home work with out distractions, like getting phone calls,and other people in the home listening to TV,or music too loud,ETC,ETC.

The second and most important reason is if a child does not understand his home work assignment WHO can he turn to to help him? Now the vast matority of children do not have anybody at home who are academicaly qualified to help them.

Now there are some parents who are academicaly qualified to help their children with home work.And some of them will simply home school their children and not send them to school.Now if you expect all parents to be academicaly qualified to help their children with their homework. Then why don't we just require them to home school their children and save billions and billions of dollars on the up keep of our schools and paying teachers salaries.

Now when teachers give children homework it should and needs to be done in school. A child should be given a study hall or study halls to do his home work in. Now pay close attention. A child given home work will then be able to totally concentrate without any outside distractions at all on doing their home work. Now if they need help on doing their homework they will be able to turn to a qualified teacher for help.

Now this will take a huge burden off of teachers and parents of trying to get children to do their home work at home. Now we will be providing our children with a totally improved enviornment in which to learn. Now don't you agree? Now we have a stupid mentality that every child that goes to high school wants to and is expected to go to college and more importantly can afford to go to college.

Parents are expected to save money so they can send their children to college in order for their children to be suceesful in their lives. The sad fact is, IS that there are an overwhelming number of college graduates that can not find jobs. Another sad fact is that people in our society think for some reason or another have a difficult time in understanding that a child can lead a very successful life with out having to go to college.

Now you are wondering how is this possible. AGAIN we have to change our present school system. After graduating from eight grade a child should be given a choice of wheather a child wants to go to college or not. Now if a child chooses to go to college we will continue to give a child the proper courses they need to allow them to go to college.

Now if a child chooses not to go to college we have to give them options of which we now do not give them to be successful after graduating from high school. We have to give our students alternate choices other than going to college in order to become successful with just a high school diploma. HOW do we do this?

Now one way is that all of our states are divided into counties. Now in the center of each county we should have a school known as a trade school. THIS is where our students after they arrive at our local schools can be bused to. Where they can be taught a trade of their choosing.

Now this is not a complete list but just a random list of the different trades a student will be able to choose from. A policeman,plumbing,carpentry, auto mechanics,electricians, barbers,or hair stylist, ETC ETC. Now of course the trade schools will have to ask and consult with local trade unions and associations to determine what their requirements are so our teachers will be able to teach our students the necessary requirments that will allow the local trade unions, associations and independent trades to hire them after they graduate.

Now the above trades can also be taught at local schools. The bottom line is that they need to be taught whether at trade school or local schools. Now the above is just a rough out line of how to give students an alternate way of which they can become successful with just a high school diploma.

Now how stupid are we? Let's say that all of our children who go to school go to college. Now just where do you think our qualified auto mec hanics,electricians,policemen, ETC,ETC. Are going to come from. Now a few examples,If your car breaks down or if you have a plumbing problem, ETC,ETC Who are you going to call? An unqualified college graduate to fix it or a qualified auto mechanic,plumber ETC,ETC to fix it.

The Bottom line is that we need people who are qualified in our trade unions to do this and they all make damn good money doing this. Now don't they? Now again we are completely stupid on how we educate our children because our present school system ONLY EMPHASIZES ACADMICS.

Now being academically smart DOES NOT and I repeat DOES NOT make a person a decent human being that will respect other human beings. One example look at all the crooked politicians we have had. It is also like stating that we have too many stupid criminals running around THAT we need to have smarter criminals running around.

Now we have dictators in this world. Now do you think that they were able to become dictators by being uneducated idiots? No they are highly educated people who have absolutely no regard for human life. Now a short history lesson. After World War One all nations that fought in World War One declared that this was the war to end all future wars. As we all know now this did not happen. Because maybe if after World War One all nations would have taught their children from first grade to twelfth grade that human life is sacred. that it is a huge sin against humanity to kill or cause any physical harm to a fellow human being,and that it is blasphemy to degrade a fellow human being.

Now if we would have done that World War Two and other Wars might not have taken place. Now when World War Two began it was started by two main nations. Germany and Japan. NOW PAY ATTENTION both nations were made of highly intelligent and educated people who had absolutely no respect for fellow human beings lives. They were not made up of uneducated idiots. NOW WERE THEY? Their leaders taught them that they were superior to other nations,races,and religions and that they should rule the world. Now by the grace of God we were able to defeat them.

Now this is what you can call a complete no brainer. This ranks above all the things I have previously stated,that needs to be done to improve our present school system. It has to be and needs to be our number one priority in changing our present school system. and that is to provide our children from the time a student steps on a school bus until he steps off a school bus at home with a safe and worry free environment in which to learn.

Now a student should not and I can not emphasize this enough, should not have to worry about being afraid of or be subjected to any physical violence, bullying or verbal harassment. WHILE GOING TO SCHOOL.

NOW PAY ATTENTION One in three student now complain about being bullied by other students who either physically or mentally abuse them. Now this should be totally unacceptable in our school systems. DON'T YOU THINK?

Now I will explain two ways on how we can prevent students from being bullied in our school system. Now teachers dont want to take the responsibialty of correcting students who act up in school and bully other kids. NOW THEY SHOULD NOT HAVE TO. Now what teachers have to do and be responsible for is to inform the principal of students that are acting up in class and are being bullies to other students.DON'T YOU THINK?

Now it is not the principals job to correct them. It is his job to inform the parent or parents. IT IS THE PARENT OR PARENTS JOB TO

CORRECT THEM. Now here are three steps to be taken to eliminate bullies from our school systems. NOW STEP ONE If a student acts up in class or bullies other students the teacher will turn them into the principal. The principal will then call the parent or parents in. He will then explain to the parent or parents that all schools have a zero tolerance of bullies and it is their job to correct their child.

Now if step one does not work. This is step two. The principal will again call in the parent or parents and explain to them that they now will be required to pay for and take their child to see a child psychiatrist to try and correct their childs behavior problem. Now if step two does not work, three strikes and your child is out of school. The principal will again call the parent or parents in and tell them that their child is banned from our school system.

It will no longer be our school systems responsibility to teach their child. It will be totally their responsibilty to teach their child by home schooling or hiring private tudors or what ever means. NUMBER TWO Now this is obviously the best way to stop children from being bullied in school is to teach them not to be bullies. It should have been taught a long time ago.It is a no brainer.

Now what we also have to do to prevent our children from becoming bullies. Is to teach our children from pre school,kindergarten,first grade to twelfth grade that a fellow student who is sitting next to you is simply a fellow human being. AND ALSO that HUMAN LIFE IS SACRED. NOW I will repeat this that HUMAN LIFE IS SACRED. And that is wrong and unacceptable to cause any physical or mental harm to a fellow human being.

Now that and what i have already stated what is wrong with our school system. You will now be able to understand the great need to change our present school system. We now have one in three students in this country that quit school. This is a sad an pathectic fact. That one in three students quit school. This is a huge national disgrace. DONT YOU THINK?

Now why do students want to quite school? The obvious fact is this. I see on TV and hear about too many cases where a student is physically abused, and or verbally abused and afraid to go to school. Now one in three students are afraid to go to school. Now when I went to school we did not have any class bullies and I never heard of any student being afraid to go to school because of class bullies.

Now as they say times change but you would think that our school system would change for the better not the worst. Now again I guess I was lucky because not only did we have teachers who knew how to teach us but simply put would not and did not tolerant any student who would act up in class or tried to be a class bully. Now here are only two cases of teenagers commiting suicide that I heard on TV there are more who do it.

Now case one two eighth-grade students hanged themselves because they were tired of being bullied at school. Case two one girl was not only mentally and physically abused by her fellow students but a couple of male students raped her. SO SHE COMMITED SUICIDE. Now words can not describe how pathetic this is.

Teenage suicide is now on the rise. WHY because students would RATHER DIE than put up with being bullied at school. Now it is a HUGE NATIONAL DISGRACE because this could have been prevented by addressing our bullying problem a long time ago. Now what i stated above and will state is a perfect example of why I stated that the matority of our American society is made up of idiots and hypocrites.

NOW Here is what happened to a California teacher who cared about human life. SHE was suspended because she reported to the police that one of her second grade students was physically bulling his classmates and threatened to bring a gun to school of which he would be able to shoot and kill his fellow classmates. NOW A SIDE NOTE. A ten year old boy got into an argument with his mother so he took a rifle that they had and shot her to death.

THE point and statement is that children are capable of squeezing a trigger on a gun and killing anybody. Now this is a sad and pathectic FACT. WE DO NOT CARE ABOUT HUMAN LIFE IN THIS COUNTRY. If we did care about human life in this country. We should have applauded and praised the teacher for trying to protect her students from being physically abused and potentially shot to death. INSTEAD OF BEING SUSPENDED. NOW DON'T YOU THINK?

Now I find this to be completey idiotic and stupid and you should too. STUDENTS now who are bullied victims are punished when they finally have had enough and decide to fight back. Now a middle-school student was expelled after he became fed up with a group of older boys who continually bullied him in the classroom and fought back. the bullies were just suspended.

Now just how pathectic is that? To punish the victims and not the bullies. Now we like to preach to people about moral values in this country. NOW DON'T WE? Now you tell me what kind of moral values we are teaching bullies. We are teaching them that it is all right for them to mentally and physically abuse their fellow students. Now you are stating that God says it is all right and approves of people to mentally and physically abuse other people.NOW ARNT YOU?

Now for all you people who say that you belive in God. It is a fact that God does not approve of this. Now you can not expect the parents of teenagers who commited suicide and the parents of the teenagers who are bullied are going to stand up and sing the song GOD BLESS AMERICA Because they know that God will not BLESS BULLYING IN THIS COUNTRY.

Now it is mind boggling to realize that we care more about whether gays should be allowed to get married or not RATHER than to come up with ways to prevent teenage bulling and teenagers commiting suicide because of it. And provide a completely and totally worry free environment for our students to go to school and learn.

Now the two ways that I have suggested to stop bullying should be installed immediately.NOW DONT YOU THINK? Now you would think that after hearing about class bulling and teenagers committing suicide because of it. THAT our politicians and American society would be totally outranged and demand that something should be done immediately that would prevent this from happening again.

Now we should have done something years ago to stop this. BUT over the last few years our priority has been to try and stop gays from getting married and still is. Now if gay people are stupid enough to get married let them.Now they say that fifty per cent of straight people who get married END UP getting a divorce. Now a lot of gay people who are allowed to get married in some states ALSO end up getting a divorce.

Now this helps our economy because it allows our divorce lawyers to make more money. RIGHT. Now this country likes to preach that this country is based on freedom of choice and religion on how we live our lives. NOW DONT WE? Now except and I do mean except if you are gay and you want to marry another gay person.

Now people say that it is morally wrong to be gay and allow gay people to get married. But that it is morally all right to own guns and let anybody shoot and kill anybody they want to and our children to be bullies YOU HYPOCRITES. The WORLD will now know what a joke our school system is and what a joke our moral values are NOW WON'T THEY?

Chapter Seven

Now when our constitution was written over two hundred years ago. It stated that we had the right to bear arms.At that time it was an intelligent thing to do.and made perfect sense to do. We needed firearms to protect ourselves from people who would act hostile toward us and be able to shoot wild animals to put food on the table in order to survive. Now our forefathers who wrote our constitution could in no way be able to predict that the day would come when we would have absolutely no practical use for firearms.NOW PAY ATTENTION. I can not over state or emphasize enough of our need to ban the sale and manufacture of fire arms in this country.

Now we are total idiots because we are too stupid to realize that what worked and made sense back then no longer makes sense to do now.Now idiots back then people rode horses to get around, So do you think that we should allow people to ride horses on our major highways now to get around?

Now that would be an idiotic thing to do now don't you think? The point is things that worked back then no longer apply to or will work in our modern society. The beliefs of the NAZI PARTY and GERMAN PEOPLE allowed the slaughter of innocent men. Women and children, Because they valued their beliefs more than they valued human life.

The Beliefs of our AMERICA SOCIETY and AMERICAN PEOPLE also allows the slaughter of innocent men,women, and children because we value our constitutional right to bear firearm more than we value human life. Now who do you think is more wrong in allowing the slaughter of innocent men women and children.Was it the old Nazi Party in their old beliefs or is it our present day American Society in our present day beliefs

Now think about this BLACK PEOPLE. You are extremely lucky that it was NOT written in our constitution that we had the right to own slaves BECAUSE if it would have been written in our constitution, You All would still be slaves today. Because people now would be saying that it is our constitutional right to own slaves.

Now one reason people claim that we need our right to bear fire arms is to protect us from foreign countries from invading us. Now it is time for people to wake up and realize that foreign countries have already invaded us with out firing a single shot. Times have changed idiots we now live in a globle society.

Now here in this country we allow people to kill off our local customers with our right to bear firearms. Now don't we ? Now our country and all countries of the world can no longer live as truly independent countries from the rest of the world. Now if countries would try to now live as truly independent countries they would be commiting economic suicide.

Countries who try to live as truly independent countries have committed economic suicide. Just look at how poor people who live in CUBA and NORTH KOREA are. Now simply put and we all have to realize this. All of our countries and individual political and religious beliefs no longer matter. What matters now is economics. Because economics now rule the world we now live in. And I thank GOD for that don't you. Because we no longer have any religious or poltical beliefs to fight over. NOW DO WE? The bottom line is that the few countries that are not economically integrated with the rest of the world can not in no way try to take on the world by themselves.

It is a huge shame that the idiots that run these countries because of their own individual political beliefs make their people suffer. Because they are too stupid to economically join the rest of the world. The bottom line is that the few countries that are not econmically integrated can not in no way try to take on the world by themselves. Now can they?

Now people in this country and people around the world have to wake up and realize that we have to quit trying to live in the past as independent countries. Those days are long gone. Now we can not and no country in the world can THRIVE as a truly independent country.

Why because we have all become financially dependent on one another. The United State has become the biggest customers and consumers of foreign products in the world. Now World War lll has already taken place with out a single shot being fired. by our army or other countries armies of the world. Our country has been invaded by foreign countries and we have invaded foreign countries.How where it counts the most financially. They say that money is the root of all evil WRONG. The love of money has saved the world. We now have an European Common Market where the countries of Europe have become financially integrated and no longer live as truly independent countries. Because they have become financially dependent on one another.

Now foreign countries are heavily invested in this country. Now it is very important for you to realize this. Just try and go out and buy a product that is made in AMERICA. The bottom line is that it is a hard thing to do.Now a few example are this the majority of breweries that make our beer are now owned by foreign countries and The small American Flags that people wave at parades are made in China.Now foreign countries are not made up of complete idiots. They are not stupid enough to want to come over here and kill off their customers,

I know it is hard to grasp and realize but we could not become a truly independent country like we were in the 40's and 50's even if we tried to. Also no major country in the world can become a truly independent country like they were in the 40's and 50's those days are long gone.

We now live in a global society. We now have the ability to have instant communication with people around the world and the ability to travel to all countries of the world. Now since we now live in a globel society we have to start thinking globel. and start treating all people of the world simply as human beings who share this planet earth.We now have to wake up and realize that we have to stop stereotyping and judging people by their race,religon,nationality, or anything else.People in this country and people who live in other countries of the world have to quit doing this. Dont you think?

Now we have to start looking at every person on this planet as a fellow human being nothing more or less, and treat everybody as being equal. Because we are all just sharing this planet earth. Now we have the communications to get this message to everybody on earth. Now dont you think we should do this?Now I could write A hundred books or more on the way thousands of innocent men,women, and children are killed because of our right to bear firearms.

These are just a few examples of how innocent people are killed because of our right to bear firearms.Now A man slept with A loaded hand gun under his pillow to protect hisself and house from intruders. Now it did not and I repeat it did not protect him from intruders. He was awaken to find an intruder standing over him with a gun pointed at his head.

Needles to say he had no opportunity to protect his self with a loaded hand gun under his pillow from an intruder who had a loaded hand gun pointing at his head. Now you hear about this all the time. A policeman who is trained to use a hand gun and openly carry one is shot to death by an idiot who has the right to carry a hand gun.

Now an off duty police man and his girl friend were sitting in his private car. He had a loaded hand gun in his glove compartment. Now even though he had a loaded hand gun in his glove compartment. He still was not able to stop an idiot with the right to bear fire arms from coming up to his car and shooting and killing him and his girlfriend to death.

Now it should be obvious to you that owning and having the right to bear firearms DOES NOT and I repeat DOES NOT give you protection from some other idiot who has the right to bear firearms. The bottom line is this owning and carring a firearm DOES NOT and I repeat DOES NOT make you BULLET PROOF.I can not emphasis that enough.Now A man who thought like a lot of you idiots do. That having a loaded hand gun in his house would protect him and his family. Now this is what happend. HIS wife wanted a divorce. But he did not want one. He wanted to try and make his marriage to her work because of the children that they had. Now the woman took the gun and shot and killed her husband. To make a long story short the police arrested her and she was sent to prison for killing her husband.

Now again people say that they have to keep guns in their house to protect themselves. Now pay attention. IN CHICAGO an aunt of a seven year old girl decided to give her niece a birthday party in her house. I am sorry to say that the seven year old girl was shot to death simply by being inside of her aunt's house. By some idiot who was outside of the aunts house with an assault weapon.

Two week before that a 14 year old girl who lived in the same neigberhood was also inside her house and was shot to death by some idiot who was outside of her home with an assault weapon. Now some idiot took an assault weapon and shot more than two dozen bullets into a house in CALUMENT CITY,ILL killing a pregnant mother,her son and critically injuring her 18 month old daughter.

NOW PAY ATTENTION PEOPLE say that they need to buy firearms and keep them in their houses to protect themselves from their fellow AMERICANS. Needless to say the above three instances absolutely proves that even if all of them kept a dozen firearms in their houses. They would not have been able to protect themselve with their right to bear firearms from other idiots who also have the right to bear firearms..

Now a person was driving his car down a street and the car crashed into a house. Why? Because the man was shot to death while driving his car. Also a man was shot and killed simply by trying to drive his car on I 65 south of INDIANAPOLIS,INDIANA. Now do you think that if they carried guns in their cars they would have been able to protect themselves from being shot to death by the idiots who shot and killed them. Obviously the answer is no.

Now this was also sad to hear about. A man in INDIANAPOLIS,INDIANA went into a house and shot and killed not just one or two people but four innocent adults and three innocent children. Why? Because of our right to bear firearms and it is so easy to pull the trigger on a gun. Now I hear about this way too often. Where teenagers are shot to death simply by trying to walk to school. Here is just one example.

An 18 year old student who was a week away from graduating from high school was shot and killed simply by trying to walk down a city street in Chicago to school. Now to honor his son's death the father showed up at his sons graduation cermony and received his dead son's diploma. Now I hear about how people like to say that everybody has the opportunity to live the GREAT AMERICAN DREAM of becoming successful in their lives.

Well sad to say thier are thousand of children and teenagers who are denied that opportunity because they shot to death because of our right to bear firearms.IDIOTS. Now when one of our soldiers are killed in Iraq we all mourn his loss and people protest the war in Iraq. Now I hear about way too many soldiers who survive serving in Iraq only to be shot to death simply by trying to walk down our cities streets in this country.

Now our nations reaction to our soldiers who survive their tour of duty in Iraq only to be shot and killed in this country. ABSOLUTELY NONE. No reaction at all because simple put we don't care Now what is completely mind bogging to me and should be to you and this country.

Is the fact we care more about our right to bear firearms than we do about human life in this country. It is also obvious that we are a nation of hypocrites. We care about foreigners killing us but we do not care about how many Americans shoot and kill other AMERICANS WHY? Because we care more about our right to bear firearms more that we do human life.

Now this is another reason people say that we need the right to bear firearms. And this is the most pathetic and ridiculous reason of all time. That is to protect ourselves against our fellow Americans. Now this reason alone proves beyond a shadow of doubt, that this countrty is made up of mostly idiots and hipocrites. Now having the right to bear firearms does not and I repeat does not protect us from our fellow Americans.

It does not prevent our fellow Americans from firing bullets at us and killing us. Simply put carring a firearm does not and I repeat does not protect us from people firing bullets at us and make us bullet proff.Now dont you agree?Now banning the sale and manufacturing of firearms and owning firearms in this country will and I repeat will not protect us from our fellow Americans.Idiots.

Now it is a national disgrace to have so little trust in our fellow Americans and GOD that we feel and believe that we should have the right to buy firearms to protect ourselves against our fellow Americans. Now if we actually had any trust in our fellow Americans and God we would ban the sale and manufactureing of firearms in this country.

Now we like to say and state that IN GOD WE TRUST, NOW GOD knows that we are hypocrites for saying that. Because we allow the slaughter by firearms 30.000 innocent men,women, and children every year to be shot to death because of our right to bear firearms. Now it is up to you the American people which motto is it going to be IN GOD WE TRUST or IN GUNS WE TRUST. The choice is yours to make.

Now God gave us brains. It is a shame that we are too stupid to use the brains that God gave us. NOW ISNT IT? Now a police officer while visiting at his farther's home was shot and killed he survived a tour of duty in Iraq only to be shot to death in this country. Now at his funeral a poltican stated that God cut his life short.

Now that is the most ridiculous statement I ever heard of against God. Now instead of putting the blame on our own stupidity because we have easy access to and the right to bear fire arms. HE BLAMED GOD. He stated it was GODS will that he was shot to death. Wow somebody should shoot and kill the Politician because he would have the perfect defense at his trial. He can simply state GOD cut his life short. RIGHT? Now if GOD would come down to earth in human form and tell us to ban the sale and manufacture of firearms we would take our guns and shoot him so full of holes that he would end up looking like a piece of swiss cheese. NOW WOULDN'T WE?

Now pay attention we the people of the good old USA have complete control of whether or not we have the right to easy access and the right to bear firearms that will allow any idiot to go out and shoot and kill innocent men,woman and children. GOD DOES NOT HAVE the power or control to ban the sale and manufacture of firearms in this country. NOW DOES HE? ONLY WE IDIOTS DO.

Now it is totally and completely wrong to blame GOD because we are too stupid to use the brains he gave us.Now this completely proves that we worship our right to bear firearms more and I repeat more then we worship GOD. Now about ten years ago a friend of mine brought a set of yard darts for us to play with. Now yard darts is where you take two small plastic circles and put them about 20 feet apart, and take four darts with sharp metal tips and try to make them stick up right in the circles of plastic.

I enjoyed playing yard darts and I told my friend I wanted to buy a set. He proceeded to tell me that they banned the sale of yard darts.Because young children were being serious hurt by playing with them.Now society bans the sale and manufacturing of yard darts and any other toys that they belive will be harmfull to children. Now I hear all the time where children are able to get hold of a hand gun and shoot and kill other children or themselves. Now you would think that our society would ban the sale and manufacturing of hand guns right. NO THEY DO NOT.

WHY? Instead society passes the responsibility on to the parents and adults to keep children away from hand guns. Now when it comes to yard darts or anything else that will cause harm to or hurt our children we ban the sale of them. But when it comes to hand guns we pass the blame on to other people. You see we dont care how many innocent children die because of hand guns now do we? Because our sacred right to bear firearms is far more importent to our society than human life.NOW ISNT IT?

Now we have a society for the prevention of cruelity to animals. Of which is mad up of hyprocrites. Why? Because they preach how wrong it is to be cruel to and to treat animals inhumanely. But they make an exception to when it comes to wild animals. NOW DON'T THEY? They don't say a damn thing about hunters who take rifles and go out and give wild animals a painful and excruciating death by shooting them.

Now if they just wounded an animal like a bird or deer.ETC. The bird will continue to fly away from you and a deer will run away from you Only to die a Slow and painful and excruciating death. You cant treat an animal or bird any more cruely than that. NOW CAN YOU? Now they have farms where they raise wild birds Lets say you want a pheasant. They will then charge you x amount of dollars for it. Now they will take the bird out of a cage and plant it in a field. They then will give you a hunting dog to help you find it and flush it out. Now hunters will be able to take their shotguns or rifles and give them a painfull and excruciating way to die by killing them or wounding them.NOW WHAT FOR IDIOTS? WHEN you can take a bird out of a cage and kill it humanely like we do cattle and pigs.

Instead hunters want to see them suffer. NOW THAT'S PATHECTIC ISN'T IT? Now what I would like to see is how many hunters we would have if we could enable wild animals to be able to fire back at hunters and be able to kill them. Now there is a way that you could say that wild animals can fight back. They could be carring a virus that could make you sick or kill you.

Bird flu is a type of virus that can kill you.Now we have to watch out for the domestic animals that we eat. They can contact any virus like mad cow disease,swine flu.rabbies. etc. Now we have total control over the way we raise domestic animals.Simply put if they contact a disease or virus that can harm us. We can prevent them from being slaughterd and eaten by us.

Because we kill them humanly we can check them out and make sure that they don't have a disease or virus that will hurt us before we eat them. Now when it comes to wild animals of which we have absolutely no control over what type of disease or virus that they have. To allow hunters to go out and shoot wild animals with out knowing what kind of disease or viruse,they have is the ultimate in stupidity. To eat something that you have no idea will kill you or not is down right stupid DON'T YOU THINK?

Now again they have farms where they raise wild birds,deer etc.Now they can have complete control over any diseases the animals they raise might get. Now they can kill them humanly and make sure that they are disease free. There is an old saying that says IT IS BETTER TO BE SAFE THAN SORRY.DON'T YOU THINK?

Now the above just proves to you that we care more about our sacred right to bear firearms than we do animal or human life. NOW DON'T WE? Now you terrorists are the most stupid and ignorant people on the planet earth. Why? Because you think that you have to come up with complicated plots to come over here and blow yourselves up to kill us Americans. When you dont have to because we are a nation of idiots and hypocrites. The following is how you can kill as many Americans you want to with guns and live to tell about it.

Now you have to realize this. We worship our right to bear fire arms more than we do God. Now you terrorists will need to be able to speak two languages English of course and Spanish. Now there are a lot of ways to enter this country. But I believe the easiest way for you to enter this country is to come up through Mexico. Now the Mexican government will give you a pamphlet telling you the safest way to enter this country.

Now if you do get caught in this country illegally the worst thing that will happen to you is that they will send you back to Mexico Where you will be able to try again. Now once you are in this country you will be able to get a low paying job. The only reason to get a low paying job is to help cover up that you are going to become a criminal who will be able to shoot and kill as many innocent people as you want to Now the smart way for you to make money illegally is to join a Spansih or English speaking street gangs, Now one of the requirements to join a street gang is this. You will be required to go out and shoot and kill somebody.Now once you join a street gang you will be able to learn how to make money by selling illegal drugs,prostitution, etc. Now you will be able to go out and form your own street gang or become an independent crimnal.

Now you terroris pay close attention. You do not even have to physically shoot and kill us.By coming over here and becoming criminals you can make millions of dollars off of selling illegal drugs,prostitution, and armed robbery etc. You can then take that money and leagally buy ship loads of firearms and then simply stand on any street in any city in the United States and pass them out. Now you can pass any rifle assault weapons or hand gun to any teenager or adult that you see and they will take them and use them to kill somebody with them.

Now when you see young children passing by do not try and give them rifles or assult weapons.They are too big for them to handle. But you can give them loaded hand guns. They then will be able to use them to kill other children themselves or adults. Now we will not even think about blaming you for giving young children loaded handguns. Because we will blame their parents for letting them have access to loaded handguns. Now just because you can get by with passing out loaded handguns to our young children.

Do not even think that you can get by with bringing in shiploads of yard darts or any other toys that are dangerous to our young children. We ban the sale and manufacturing of toys that are dangerous to our young children and we will spend billions of dollars to track you down and nail you for that if you try to do that. Now remember it is all right to give out loaded hand guns. But absolutely no dangerous toys that could harm our young children.

Now after giving out all the free firearms to us.All you have to do is sit back and watch your local news station and hear about the increase in murders in your local area. Now if you want to personally kill us. Here are some of the ways to do it. You can do this by yourself but it will be easier to do it with a fellow criminal to help you. Now you can take a car ride and do drive by shootings where if you see somebody walking down the street you simply shoot and kill them.

Now if you don't see anybody on the street to shoot and kill you just stop by any house and take out an assault weapon and fire into the house and kill anybody inside it. Now if nobody is on the street or at home There are always traffic on the streets of which you will be able to shoot and kill anybody driving a car down the street. Now when you know that people are at home. You just wait until they are asleep and put silencers on your hand guns and shoot and kill them.

Now their neighbors won't be able to hear you do that.

Now you terrorist are lucky people because people in this country believe that if they carry and have fire arms it will make them bulletproof. Now of course other people have and you will to be able to show them that they are complete idiots for thinking this. Because you will and anybody else will be able to shoot and kill them long before they have any chance of using their guns against you or anybody else.

Now you do not have to worry about people getting angry or upset about you or anybody else shooting and killing people. In this country we do not care. You have to understand this we care more about our constitutional right to bear firearms than we do human life. Like innocent children teenagers or adult life. You killing us by shooting us will only result in a TV news blimp on our local TV news channels

Now you can also shoot and kill us by going hunting. You can go hunting and claim that you accidentally shot and killed a fellow hunter while you were trying to shoot a harmless deer or other harmless animals.

We will not care. Now you terrorists think that you have to die in order to have sex with virgins. You do not have to die to have sex with virgins while living in this country. You can have sex with as many virgins that you can find.

You just take a handgun and force them to have sex with you. After you have sex with her you just shoot and kill her. Now nobody will care. She will just become A woman who was shot to death on our local TV news program. Now you can take A hand gun and you will be able to rob any bank,any store, and anybody you see walking down the street or hyjack any

How to save billions and billions of tax dollars and thousands
and thousands of innocent children, women and men's lives

51

car that you want. Now it would be real difficult for you to try and do this without a handgun.

Now because of our constitutioal right to bear firearms. We make it as easy as possible for people to become criminals with the use of handguns. Now after what happened in TUCSON AR. You terrorists need to know this. DO NOT and I repeat DO NOT shoot and try to kill a politician. Now six people were killed and 14 wounded A politician was wounded. Now even though the gunman was caught right away the FBI was sent to investigate it because a politician was shot and wounded. Now a nine year old girl was shot to death along with five other people.

Now if the 9 year old girl and five other people would have been the only ones killed. It would not have been a national news story. Four days after that happened a 14 year old boy was shot to death in Chicago. It did not make any national news. No FBI investigation. The bottom line is we do not care how many thousands of innocent children woman and men are shot to death in this country. So you can shoot as many of them as you want to. Just do not shoot and kill a politician. Because we believe that there lives are far more valuable than innocent children, women, and men's lives.

Now if you shoot and kill just three people a day which is no big deal in our major cities. Now that comes to over a 1,000 people a year. Now why just kill three people a day. Because nobody will care or notice in our major cities. Now if just 1,000 of you come over hear and spread yourselves out over our major cities and just kill three people a day. It will add up to 1,000,000 people a year. And nobody but nobody will care.

Now I have to warn you terrorist. When you are here and are driving a car You better make damn sure you are wearing a seat belt. We will nail you if you dont. Because that is our police officers number one priority. Now trying to protect us from criminals like you takes a back seat as they say. Now there are a lot of instances where people are killed in a car accident because they were wearing seat belts.

Now understand this our government does not give us a choice of whether to wear a seat belt or not. Our government insists that we die with our seat belts on. Remember now when you are driving a car our police force will be watching you. To make sure you are wearing your seat belts. The bottom line is when you want to go out and do your drive by shootings. Just make damn sure you are wearing your seat belts and you will be okay.

Now you terrorits need to set up a retirement program for yourselves. Do not become too selfish or greedy. Now after twenty years of killing thousand of innocent people and making millions of dollars off of selling illegal drugs, prostitution, armed robbery etc. You need to retire and let younger terrorits come over here and do the same thing. Now lets say that you are 21 years old when you come over here.

Now after 20 years you will be able to retire at the age of 41 years. That will give you at least 30 years of retirement of which you will be 71 years old. Of which you will be able to spend all that time living in the lap of luxury living in any place in the world that you want to. Now honest hard working people in this country in order to get full retirement benefits have to work their ass off until they are 65 years old. Now they want to pass legislation to require you to be 70 years old to receive full benefits.

Now don't you terrorist think that coming over here and becoming criminals and be able to make a ton of money. Shoot and kill thousand of Americans and live a long life.Instead of coming over here and blowing yourself up. Is the most profitable and safest way to kill us.

Now since I have proven to you that owning and having firearms does not make you bullet proof or are able to protect yourself from somebody else having a firearm. I believe the safest and most effective way to protect myself against my fellow Americans is to own nuclear arms. Now I will prefer to buy nuclear missiles which will be easy to fire.

Now our government has to sell me nuclear missiles. Why?Because is my constitutional right to bear arms and our supreme court has stated this. Now when our costitution was written it does not ban the ownership of nuclear arms or automatic weapons,assault rifles etc. Now does it. Now people say firearms do not kill people but people kill people. Right? Now pay attention nuclear missiles do not kill people but people kill people. Right?

Now if I really get scared of my fellow Americans and set off a nuclear missile that kills a couple of million people or more. I am positive that nobody will care because of my constitutional right to bear arms. Why? Because we now allow thousand and thousands of innocent men,women, and children to be killed because of our constitutional right to bear firearms. The simple fact is that we care more about our constitutional right to bear firearms than we do human life, NOW DONT WE?

Now they had a program on TV where they took six people and gave them training on how to use and carry a hand gun. They put each of them one at a time in a large class room with other people in it. Now a man enters the room and starts shooting at the people in the room and at the person carring a hand gun. Now the person carring a handgun was not able to react in time to stop the person from shooting at him and killing him.

Now the other five people who were put in the same situation were also unable to react in time to prevent the man shooting at them from killing them. Now i can not emphasize this enough, Carring a gun does not make you bullet proof. They also stated that 30,000 innocent children teenagers and adults are shot to death on a yearly basis.

NOW WAKE UP PEOPLE If a criminal is going to rob your home the vast majority will do it when you are not at home. Now if you have firearms in your house. They will rob you of them and use them to kill or rob other people. Now if you are at home unless a criminal is a complete idiot. He will us a gun to break into your home while your are sleeping. Now as I stated before if a man who slept with a gun under his pillow was unable to stop a criminal from breaking into his house and robbing him. Now What kind of a chance do you think that you will have of protecting yourself from a criminal who enters your home with a gun while you are sleeping. ABSOLUTEY NONE. Now people still mourn the loss of 3,000 people who were killed from 9/11 and rightly so. Now just in the year of 2007 alone over 8,000 children were wounded by firearms and 2,000 children were killed. Now nobody but nobody mourns the loss of 2,000 children who were killed by firearms. Now do they?

Now the complete and total apathy and indiference by the American people is mind boggling, To Know that American people care more about their right to bear firearms more than they do innocent children lives is TOTALLY PATHETIC, LIKE I stated before we are a nation of idiots and hypocrites. Now if you want to protect yourselves against your fellow Americans. The way to do it being that nobody will have any firearms is to use baseball bats and guard dogs.

Now you can openly keep baseball bats anywhere you want to in your house. Now children,teeagers,and adults will be able to pick up a baseball bat and beat the hell out of an intruder. Now a guard dog needs only to bark up a storm when an intruder shows up and the intruder will turn around and run away. Now you will be able to take baseball bats and guard dogs to anyplace you want to go.

Now people will say that if we ban the sale and manufacturing of firearms.That only criminals will have them.WRONG NOW if a person is caught having a firearm. He will be fined 30,000 dollars or more. Now if a person knows somebody that has a firearm and turns them into police.

The police will then be able to get a search warrent and search the house for a firearm.

Now if the police find a firearm in the house. The person who has the firearm will have to pay a 30,000 dollar fine. Now the person who turned him in will be able to collect a reward of 15,000 dollars tax free. Now the person who turned him in will be and remain anonymous. That means that the person who has the firearms will never be able to know or find out who turned him in.

Therefore a good friend or relative will be able to and want to turn him in and not have to worry about him being able to know that they turned him in. Now when people see a criminal commit a crime with a gun they will not look the other way. They will want to track him down and see where he goes. So they can call the police and collect the 15,000 reward. NOW WONT THEY?

Now a ten year old boy got into an argument with his mother. So he went and got a 22 caliber rifle that they kept in their house and shot and killed his mother. Now he is standing trial for murdering his mother. Now we should stand up and hail our right to bear firearms for makeing it easy for children to be able to shoot and kill people for what ever reason they want to.

Now here is more proof that by carring a gun does not make you bullet proof. Now a man was able to walk into a police station and shoot four policemen before other policemen were able to react and shoot and kill him. Now a man snapped at his place of work and took his rage out on his fellow co-workers. He took a gun and killed eight of his fellow co-workers and him self.

Now if he would have been a terrorist and blew his self and eight people up. Our whole country would have been up in arms about it. No pun intended. We would have demanded that our government do something about it. Now because of our sacred right to bear firearms, Nobody but nobody cared about it. It was just a news blimp on T.V. Now just how pathetic is that. YOU HYPOCRITES? Now here is more proof that the majority of the people in this country is made up of the idiots and hyprocrites.

Now our whole nation was upset because a gunman in TUCSON ARIZONA shot to death 6 people one who was a 9 year old girl and wounded 14 other people one who was a politician. Now we did not or were upset because a 9 year old girl was shot to death BECAUSE four days after that a 14 year old boy was shot to death in Chicago and our nation did not care.

Thousands of children have been shot to death before that and our nation has not cared. What upset our nation and especially our politicians was that a politician was wounded. Our president went there to console the wounded politican and her family. WHY? HIM and other politicians have never cared about how many innocent children,women and men wounded before this. NOW HAVE THEY?

The gunman that did this was caught. He had no previous criminal record. So why was the FBI sent there to investigate the case. THEY do not investigate other shootings. NOW DO THEY? They tried to find a political reason for the shootings because a politician was wounded. Now obviously and simply put they they will not find any reason other than the real reason for the killings our right to bear firearms. The gunman snapped and become a mental case for what ever reason. And went out and bought a gun decided to shoot and kill people.

Now this has happened thousand of times before where a person with no criminal record has snapped and for what ever reason has taken a gun and shot and killed a person or multiple people. And will happen again in the future. Now politicians have decided to become psychologists. They are trying to put the blame on each others political beliefs. As the reason the gunman shot and killed 6 people and wounded 14.

Now this is what you can call unbelievable stupidity. Obviously they are way to stupid to realize that you can not stop anybody from buying a gun and going out and shooting and killing a person or multiple people. BECAUSE of our sacred right to bear firearms. This proves beyond a shadow of doubt that this country absolutely does not have any compassion for human life.

We do not care how many innocent human lives we have to sacrifice for our sacared right to bear fire arms. NOW DO WE? Now how stupid is this country? We all refuse to and will not put the blame where it obviously belongs on our right to bear firearms. NOW THINK ABOUT THIS IF we would have banned the sale and manufacturing of fire arms. Those five people and the nine year old girl would still be alive today. NOW WOULDNT THEY?

Now politicians want to try and come up with laws that would protect them from being shot to death. One politician suggested that a person with a gun not be allowed to carry it within a thousand feet of a politician. Now they do not care how many thousands of innocent lives are sacrificed for our right to bear firearms.

They want to try and make sure that their lives are not sacrificed for our right to bear firearms. THINK ABOUT THAT.NOW PAY ATTENTION TO ALL CHILDREN AN TEENAGERS THAT LIVE IN THIS COUNTRY. You have to ask your parents,teachers and any adult why they believe in our right to bear firearms more than they do your life. Why they are willing to sacrifice your life and consinder your life to be meaningless when it comes to our right to bear firearms.

You also need to ask your parents,teachers and any adult why they dont want to vote to ban firearms. BECAUSE if they did vote to ban firearms. they would prevent and make absolutely sure that you would not have to worry about being shot to death. Now you need to write or mail our politicians and ask them to explain that why when it comes to our right to bear firearms that they consinder their lives as being valuable and worth trying to protect and consider your life as being worthless and not worth trying to protect

Now people want to deny MUSLIMS their right to worship their God. They want to try and stop them from building mosques to worship their God. They want to deny MUSLIMS their constitutional right of freedom of religion. WHY? Because they believe that their God wants them to go out and blow themselves and other people up and kill them in his name. NOW PAY ATTENTION IDIOTS IF all MUSLIMS believe that their God wants them to go out and blow themselves up.

Eventually there would be nobody left to worship him. Now you idiots believe that their God wants to end up with nobody left to worship him. RIGHT? Now you idiots believe that our God approves of people going out and shooting and killing thousands if innocent children,teenagers,women and men. BECAUSE of our right to bear firearms. Talk about being stupid. you would have to be complete idiots to believe that our God would approve of seeing thousands and thousands of innocent people being shot to death that worship him. Now when 9/11 happened 3,000 people were killed.

Now 9 years later 270,000 people have been shot to death in this country. Now Muslims have a long way to go catch up with us in killing Americans. NOW DONT THEY? NOW we do a damn good job of killing each other off without any help from Muslims. NOW DONT WE?Now there are people who live in this country who are totally honest about their beliefs. They say and state that they do not believe in God. This is a free country and they have every right not to.

Now this is for people who live in this country and state that they believe in God. Now we have a national motto that states IN GOD WE TRUST.

And people love to state GOD BLESS AMERICA. NOW DON'T WE? The majority of people who live in this country state that they believe in God. That is a national joke. Now people like to say and state that they believe in God but they really don't. Now pay attention all politicians state that they believe in God, WHY? because there is no way they would be able to get elected if they stated that they did not. The point is we could have a lot of politicians who don't believe in God and we would have no way of knowing that. NOW WOULD WE?

Now politicians state that people have the right to carry firearms into churches and people do carry firearms into churches. Now politicians and people who carry firearms into churches are making a clear cut statement that they worship and have more trust in firearms that they do God. NOW DON'T THEY? Now I assume because I don't know for sure that politician and people who carry guns into churches are playing right into the devils hands.

AND DO NOT REALIZE THIS. THEN AGAIN MAYBE THEY DO. Now it makes the devil a very happy camper to know that people worship and have more trust in their firearms more than they have trust in God. Now the only safe place to worship God is to rent an airplane at your local airport or go to your local court house where our government bans people from carrying firearms into them.

Now people can no longer feel safe going to church because of people carring firearms to church. Now you hear about this all the time on TV where a person with no previous criminal record will snap and flip out and kill innocent people with a gun. The bottom line is you can not completely trust people who carry a gun because you can not know when or if they are going to snap and flip out and shoot you. THINK ABOUT THIS HOW many times have you heard people say the devil made me do it.

Now all of you people who want to carry firearms into churches and other people who carry firearms. You all obviously worship firearms more than you do God. Therefore you really should build your own temples where you will be able to worship your firearms and the devil without endangering people who worship God more than they do firearms. You all will have a great time worrying about who is going to snap and shoot you. You need to realize this carrying a firearm does not make you BULLET PROOF.

Now think long and hard about this. Who do you think benefits the most from our right to bear firearms? God or the devil? Now the DEVIL loves to see innocent children,women and men who worship God be shot to death because of our right to bear firearms, NOW DOSN'T HE? Now do you really think that GOD approves of seeing thousands and thousands of innocent people who worship him being shot to death because of our right to bear firearms. NOW DO YOU.

Now seeing thousand and thousand of innocent children,women,and men who worship god being continously shot to death. Obviously makes the DEVIL very happy. Now the devil is very thankfull that we have the right to bear firearms in this country and does not want to see us ban firearms in this country. NOW DOSE HE. Now how in the world can you expect and even want God to bless a country that allows thousands and thousands of innocent children,women,and men who worship him to be continously shot to death.

Simply because of our right to bear arms. Now you have no moral right to expect God to bless this country. NOW DO YOU? The bottom line is this are we going to continue to please the devil or ban the sale and manufacturing of firearms and please God. The choice is yours to make. NOW PAY ATTENTION THIS IS THE BEST COUNTRY IN THE WORLD TO LIVE IN. WHY? BECAUSE we have the RIGHT to be total and complete IDIOTS AND HYPOCRITES.

To be able to belive in God or not and to be able to go out and buy a gun and go out and shoot anybody they want to LIKE policemen. A 14 year old boy being shot to death in a hunting accident, and two young women a 19 year old and a 17 year old their bodies were found in a wooden area outside of the town where they lived. One of them had a one year old daughter who now gets to grow up without a loving mother to take care of her

Now president Obama and he is not the only politician to make the following statements. SACRIFICE FOR THE COMMION GOOD. Now if politicians realy believed that they would ban the sale and manufacture of firearms. NOW WOULDNT THEY? Now the greatness of our country is the liberty to pursue our dreams NOW they leave out one important statement UNLESS of course you are one of the thousands and thousands of innocent children,women and men who are shot to death. on a continuous basis because of our constitutional right to bear firearms. They keep forgetting to make that follow up statement. NOW DON'T THEY?

Now we are making a huge statement to the millions of living innocent children and teenagers and other people in this country. AND THAT IS

THIS THAT we do not care about human life in this great country of ours. We could care less whether you live or die. We callously sit back and watch you being shot to death. We have absolutely no national protest about it being done, NOW DO WE ? Now our total indifference to this fact is truly mind boggling and amazing isnt it?

Obviously we believe that human life is meaningless and insignificant compared to our right to bear and worship firearms. NOW ISNT IT?

Simply put we do not care or give a damn about how many thousands of innocent children,teenagers and other innocent people that we allow and let be shot to death and sacrificed for our right to bear and worship our firearms. NOW DO WE?

NOW YOU TERRORISTS PAY ATTENTION. You do not need to try and come over here and blow yourselves up or kill us with guns trying to kill innocent American lives. Just sit back and watch us do it. We really do not need your help in killing innocent Americans. We do a damn good job of doing that all by ourselves. You see we do not care how many human sacrifices we have to make no amount is too great for us to give up our right to bear firearms.

Now the vast majority of Americans say that they believe in God. Now if you truly believe in GOD YOU will do everything in your power to protect human life. NOW WONT YOU? Now this is a free country we live in and you do not have to believe in GOD. But you should believe that human life is sacred unless you believe that it is all right for somebody to shoot and KILL YOU.

NOW simply put we will be able to find out if the vast majority of Americans truly belive in GOD OR NOT. Now only you can decide which of the following statements are going to be true or not. Is our national motto going to continue to be IN GOD WE TRUST or IN GUNS WE TRUST and our we going to be able to say with a clear conscience GUNS BLESS AMERICA or GOD BLESS AMERICA.

Now do you want to make GOD HAPPY or the DEVIL HAPPY? The clear cut choice is yours to make. Now pay close attention. It should be obvious to you that GOD is motivating me and wants me to write this book. It is also obvious that the devil does not want me to write this book. NOW DOES HE?

Now our government states that you can not bring firearms to an airport or carry them on a plane al so you can not carry them into a courthouse. Why? Because by denying prople their consitutional right to bear firearms at airports,courthouse or carry them on air planes. It saves thousands of innocent men women and children lives it stops people from being able to hyjack an airplane and kill hundreds of innocent people lives on the airplanes.

Now it is an awesome feeling for people to be able to go to airports and courthouses and not have to worry about themselves or children being shot to death by some idiot with a gun. NOW ISNT IT? Now when it comes to individual cities that also want to save thousands of innocent men,women,and childrens lives by banning firearms in their cities. GUESS WHAT? Our government steps in and says you can not do that.

Why? Because our government states that cities have absolutely no legal right to deny our constitutional right to bear firearms. Also our supreme court has ruled that we have our constitution right to bear firearms. Therefore our goverment has no legal or constitutional right to ban people from carring firearms at airports on airplanes or in court houses. NOW DO THEY?

Now pay attention when our constitution was written over 200 years ago it stated that we have the right to bear firearms. It does not state EXCEPT at airports or on airplanes or in courthouses. NOW DOES IT? Now our forefathers had had absolutely no way to be able to predict that the day would come when we would have absolutely no practical use for firearms or that the day would come when the only thing that we used them for was to kill innocent men,women and children commit armed robbery and be able to rape innocent women. etc. they would have banned our right to bear firearms. NOW WOULDNT THEY?

Now you have to wake up and realize this idiots. It costs us taxpayers billions and billions of dollars to prosecute people for the illegal use of firearms. Now when we convict people of murdering innocent men,women, and children. We give them life sentences and long periods of time for armed robbery etc. Now for every year that we keep them in jail. It costs us billions and billions of dollars to do so.

Now as you know a lot of teachers,policemen and other people etc. have been and are being laid off. Now a lot of them have mortgages of which they will no longer be able to make payments on them and lose their homes. Now they will have to tell their children that even though we are homeless and that we have less teachers to give you a good education,less policemen to protect you and that when you grow up you will have a hard time finding a job.

You will still have our constitutional right to own and carry firearms because we believe that you can not trust your FELLOW AMERICANS

How to save billions and billions of tax dollars and thousands and thousands of innocent children, women and men's lives

61

OR GOD. Now if we ban the manufacturing and sale of firearms. Here are some of the things that we can do with the billions and billions of dollars that we can save every year. Now we some of the billions of dollars into our social security retirement fund. So people could be able to retire will full benfits at age 62.

Also be able to extend unemployment benefits and hire more teachers policemen and create more jobs for other people, and lower state income taxes sales,sales taxes, personal property taxes,etc. Now think long and hard about that. Now in summation If we DO NOT go out and vote to ban the sale and manufacturing of firearms in this country. SIMPLY PUT YOU will prove to the rest of the world that we are truly idiots and hypocrites. Now if you try and state that we believe in GOD WE TRUST and GOS BLESS AMERICA the World will laugh at us.Those mottos will now become a HUGE WORLD WIDE JOKE.

Now by banning guns you can prvent somebody from shooting and killing a spouse, one of your children or a friend. Now if you do not vote to ban guns Then you will be able to explain to your spouse, your children and friends WHY? That you value your right to bear firearms more that you do their lives. And if need be sacrifice their lives. AND ALSO allow the government to have to waste billions and billions of tax dollars. Now you really need to think long and hard about the great need to ban firearms. Because it will be a huge and I do mean huge benefit to you and your family to ban firearms.

Now after I wrote the above chapter on why we need to ban firearms I found out about two hard facts that you need to know about.

. One The risk of suicide is up to 10 TIMES GREATER in homes with guns. Now people with suicidal feelings often pass quickly. But having easy access to firearms can turn a temporary condition into A permanet tragedy. Now not only will A person just snap and kill himself. NOW YOU hear about this all the time don't you. A person will take A firearm and shoot and kill other people and then shoot and kill themselves. NOW WONT THEY?

TWO The risk of homicide is 3 times greater in homes with guns. Now that is a very hard fact to try and completely ignor. NOW ISN'T IT?

NOW it should be perfectly clear and obvious that it is totally pointless to own and keep guns in your home. Unless you do not care about putting your spouse and children at a higher risk of being shot to death. NOW PAY CLOSE ATTENTION. KNOCK KNOCK who's there? IDIOTS WHAT IDIOTS? IDIOTS that will still want to keep guns in their home.

Knowing that hard facts has proven that keeping firearms in your house increases the risk of you and your family of being shot to death.

Now I thank God that when I grew up and later got married and raised my kids THAT the vast majority of Americans trusted in GOD and their fellow Americans. They did not feel the need to go out and buy guns to keep in their homes and carry them where ever they went. Now as they say times have changed, Now nobody has absolutely no trust in God or their fellow Americans, NOW DO THEY?

Now I will explain to you what people can do with our constitutional right to bear arms.First off we have a constitutional right to carry fire arms on airlines and in court houses.OUR government has no legal right to go against our constitutional right to bear arms, Now do they? Now I can assume that a lot of people are afraid to fly or go in our court houses. Because they are not allowed to carry fire arms with them to be able to protect them selves against their untrust worthy fellow Americans RIGHT.

NOW if you want to kill a person who carries a gun This is how you can do it without having to worry about going to jail. Now first off you have to make sure that you are totally alone with him. Now when you first see him make sure that you have your hand on your concealed gun. Then you pull it out now let him go for his gun and when he has it in his hand you just shoot and kill him. Now if he does not have his gun out you can go ahead and shoot and kill him anyway. After you kill him you just take his gun out put it in his hand. Now of course make sure you use gloves to do it.

Now make sure that you carry a cell phone so you can call the police right away. Now when the police get there all you have to do is tell the police that he pulled a gun on you and that you were able to shoot him before he was able to shoot you. You now have a perfect case of self defense. Now you have to realize this people who carry guns ABSOULELY believe that by carrying a gun it will make them bullet proof.

NOW if a person dose not have a concealed firearm on him. YOU can go ahead and shoot and kill him. Now call the police. Now you just explain to the police that since we no longer have any trust in GOD or our fellow Americans and just worship our firearms. that you had to assume that he had one. Now the police will have no choice but to agree with you. and you can claim self defense. And you tell them thank goodness for our constitutional right to bear firearms. That allows us to shoot and kill anybody that threatens us unarmed or armed people.

NOW for people who are married go out and buy two hand guns and also buy a large life insurance policy on your spouse. Now if you end up

How to save billions and billions of tax dollars and thousands and thousands of innocent children, women and men's lives

63

not getting along instead of getting a divorce. You just take a gun and shoot and kill him or her. You then take the other gun and place it in his or hers hand. Now you call the police. Now you explain to the police that you and your spouse decided that you both should carry guns around your house to protect yourself against untrust worthy fellow Americans,

Now you tell them that you got into a big fight and that your spounce threaten you with his or her gun and that you were lucky enough to be able to shoot and kill your spouce before your spouse was able to shoot and kill you. A perfect case of self defense. Now Don't you think it was awfully nice of me to show you how to kill any body you want to and not go to jail for doing it.

Now if after reading what i just stated about the total stupidity of having the right to bear arms and you DO NOT BAN GUNS THIS will then prove to GOD that you believe in and worship firearms absolutely more than you do him. IT will also prove that we have absolutely no regard for or respect for human life in this country.Now you will prove beyond a shadow of doubt that my opening statement of this book that the majority of Americans are IDOTS AND HYPOCRITES IS ABSOLUTELY TRUE.

Chapter Eight

Now what a huge joke our politicians are. THE SAD FACT IS THIS. The majority of politicians are out just for themselves. The are not for the avarage American people they claim to be for. Now here is a perfect example. They will vote to give themselves pay raises but when it comes to voting to raise our national minimum wage law THEY HAVE VOTED AGAINST IT.

Now it is obvious that they do not care about millions of American people who have to work for minimum wages. NOW DO THEY? Now the majority of politicians are two faced hypocrites. They will say what ever the people want to hear to get elected or reelected. NOW WONT THEY? Now when it comes to voting for bills in congress this is what they do.

They will vote for bills that will benefit themselves, rich people, special interest groups, and lobbyists. BUT when it comes to voting for bills that will benefit millions of Americans they will vote against them NOW WONT THEY? Now Republicans insist on giving tax breaks to rich people, Now the first idiotic reason they come up with. WAS THIS. By giving tax break to rich people it would have a big trickle down effect on our economy. Now since that didnt work they have come up with another idiotic reason. They now state that rich people have become job creators.

Now this is what I want to know and you should too. Give us some hard facts. LIKE How many new jobs they have been able to create and will continue to be able to create by giving rich people tax breaks. OBVIOUSLY They won't be able to do this. Now it can not become more obvious than this. BY giving tax breaks to rich people.

It allows them to be able to afford to give millions of dollars to Republican Campaign Funds. NOW DON'T YOU AGREE. NOW This absolute proof that Republicans do not care if the majority of Americans live or die or have jobs or not. Now when it comes to health care reform the Republicans are totally against it. Now they also want to cut medicare benefits. Now the vast majority of Americans Appreciate the sacrifices our veterans made for this country. Now Republicans and other politicians want to cut medical benefits and pension plans for our veterans.

Now this should be a huge wake up call this proves that Republicans will go to any extent necessary to make sure that they can afford to give tax breaks to rich people.Now since rich people and Republicans can afford to pay for the best medical coverage in this country. We should only allow rich people and Republicans to join our armed forces because then we will not have to pay them any health care benefits or pension benefits. NOW DON'T YOU THINK?

Now in Canada and other countries they give free medical coverage to their citizens.Now in this country people have to pay for their medical coverage and are having a difficult time in trying to pay for it. Now obviously our politicians do not realize or are too stupid to know that 70 percent of our ecomony is based on consumer goods.

Now the more people have to pay for health care will result in more people having less money to buy consumer goods. OF WHICH will obviously result in more unemployment.. Now it is also obvious that if they do know that 70 percent of our economy is based on consumer goods.That they do not give a damn about how many people become unemployed and that it is obvious that they will do what ever it takes to give tax breaks to rich people and corporations

Now since Republicans claim that rich people are job creators Then it is obvious that we need more rich people to create jobs.So how do we do this? Easy we simply have Republicans and rich people donate 2 million dollars a year into a fund. Now out of that fund we will then randomly pick out 10,000 poor people or more and make them rich people.

Now since it is my idea I should be the first one they make rich.NOW DON'T YOU AGREE? Now that will give us 10,000 new job creators a year and after 10 years that will be 100,000 new job creators. Now I am sure that Republicans and rich people will do this to help turn our ecomomy around. RIGHT?

THE BOTTOM LINE IS THIS. RICH PEOPLE.special interest groups and lobbyists are able to donate huge sums of money to politicians election and reelection funds. Now how much money can the average voter donate to their campaign funds? Not that much money now can they?

Now the smart thing to do is this. Put a limit on how much money a politician can have in his campaign fun to get elected or relected. NOW DON'T YOU THINK? Now we have to many career politicians. Now what we have to do is this. Limit the time a person can spend as a politician. How do we do that you ask? Well we limit a politician to only be able to run for TWO terms as being president of his country. NOW DON'T WE?

Now we need to limit a politician to two terms as a senator and to two terms as a house of representative.DONT YOU THINK? This will make it a lot harder for rich people,special interest group and lobbyist to be able to have a politician in their hip pocket. NOW WON'T IT? Now we really need to have an independent party.WHY?because basically we only have the Republicans and Democrates to vote for.We really need to have other canidates to vote for.NOW DON'T YOU THINK?Now we should vote for the best candidate to represent us in congress. But we do not do that now do we? What we do is this. We will blindly vote for a Republican or a Democrates.

Why? Because people will say I always vote for A Republican or a Democrates. Now Republicans or Democrate could take a person out of a mental hospital.And what you can call a certified nut job. Now they can take him and put Him on a Republican or Democrates ticket and staunch Republicans or Democrates would vote for him. NOW WOULD'T THEY?

Now we need voters to stop being staunch Republicans or Democrates and blindly voting for Democrats and Republican you need to vote for the best candidate and not a certified nut job just because he is a Republican or Democrate. Now the majority of our politicians are hypocrites and here is proof positive. When we send Republicans and Democrates to congress now they are supposed to vote for what is best for the majority of American people. That is what they say that are going to do.NOW DON'T THEY? But when they get in to congress it all becomes about Republicans and Democrates fighting over which party is going to dictate on how this country is going to be run.NOW DON'T THEY?

What happened to the voters of this country dictating how this country should be run. Now you see it should not matter whether how many Republicans or Democrates we have in congress. They are supposed to be there to vote for what benefits the majority of American people. But they don't do that NOW DO THEY? That is why we need to put in a third party that will vote for what is best for the American people. NOW DON'T YOU THINK?

Now I can not impress this enough. We now live in a global society. Which is now run by a global economy. Our country and all major nations of the world are now economically integrated. We now have cell phones and computers which allows us to have instant communications with other people of the world. We also have the ability to be able to travel to other countries of the world.

Now 40 or 50 years ago we could not do this.NOW COULD WE? Now go out and try to buy something that is made in America. Now realize this the small American flag that people like to wave at parades and other events are made in China. Now a lot of our local breweries are owned by foreign companies. Now that is just a few examples of how we have been financially taken over by foreign countries. Now people in this country need to realize that we can no longer live like we did 40 or 50 years ago.

The huge problem we now have in this. The majority of Americans are still trying to live like we did in the past. Tmes have changed and we all have to start living in the present. You have to realize this. We can not change the past but we can change the present and future to make this a better country to live in. NOW CAN'T WE ?

Now I have stated how we can save billions and billions of tax payers dollars. Now of course it is up to you tax payers to wake the hell up and make the necessary changes to do it. Now there is one more way that we can save billions and billions of tax payers dollars and that is to cut back on our national defense spending.We now spend close to 800 billions on national defense.

Now that is close to a trillion dollars. Now that money is totally and completely wasted. Now we need to set a limit on the amount of money we totally and completely waste on national defense DON'T YOU THINK? Now 500 billion dollars should be the limit. That is half a trillion dollars to waste on our national defense.

Now I will explain to you why it is a total and complete waste to spend that much money on our national defense. Now 40 or 50 years ago spending that much money on our national defense we would have able to justify doing that. But times have changed since then. We now can no longer justify spending billions of dollars on our national defense.

Again now all that money we now spend on our national defense is a total and complete waste of money. WHY? Because it has not stopped and I repeat it has not stopped foreign countries from invading us. You have to wake up and realize this. FOREIGN COUNTRIES HAVE ALREADY

TAKEN US OVER. NOW WHERE it counts the most not physically but economically.

You now have to realize this. We as a nation of over 300 million people have become the worlds best customer of foreign goods. Now foreign countries are not and I repeat not idiots. They will not try to come over here and kill off their best customers. NOW WILL THEY? They will also help to protect us from any foreign country that would try to kill us.

Now wake up people. THE BOTTOM LINE IS THIS. When our economy thrives their economy will thrive. Now when our economy takes a dump their econormy will take a dump. Now I can not emphasize this enough. We now live in a global society run by global economics. Now we are spending close to a trillion dollars on our national defense and that is totally ridiculous. DON'T YOU THINK? Now by limiting our defense budget to 500 billion dollars we will be able to save 300 billion dollars a year. Now there are a lot of things that we can do with the trillion and billions that I have just stated that we can save only if we use our brains to do it.

Now here is a way that we can turn our economy completey around with the billions of dollars that we can save by doing what I have just showed you how to do it. We need to increase SOCIAL SECURITY BENEFITS. Now I am not talking about thousands of dollars of an increase a month. I am talking about mere 800.00 dollars a month.Now this will not result in a trickle down effect but will result in an opening of the flood gates effect. This is have a huge and I do mean huge economic impact. The will now be able to buy more consumer goods of which they will do because they will then be able to live a more comfortable life. NOW WON'T THEY? Unlike tax breaks to millionairs who already have all the consumer goods that they need.

Now realize this. It did not do the Egyptian Pharaohs any good to take their wealth with them to their graves. NOW DID IT? Now this will result in huge snowball effect. The more consumer goods that they will be able to buy will put more people to work. Now they will buy more consumer goods which will create even more jobs,etc,ect. Now I know that this will cost us billions of dollars to do.

So where will we get the billions of dollars to initially do this? Simply by legalizing drugs and prostituton,banning firearms, and cutting our defense buget and have rich people and corporations pay their fair share of taxes. How will we be able to continue to do this? Understand this. More people we put to work the more people we will have paying federal and state tax and Social Security tax. NOW WONT WE? Now this will result in people paying billions and billions of dollars into federal state and Social Security taxes of which we will not only be able to pay for the increase in Social Security benefits every year but we will have more money left to create even more jobs. Now wake up you now have a choice to make. Simply put by doing what I just stated it will allow you to be able to work and put a roof over heads for your family or be out of work and homeless. The choice is your to make.

Now here is a perfect example of how rich people by making millions of dollars in contributions to our politicians funds are able to run our country. Now some of our major banks in this country were on the verge of going bankrupt. Now how did the banks get the goverment to spend over 700 billion dollars to bail them out. Simply put they donate millions of dollars to individual politicians campaign funds and our politicians can be bought off by rich people so rich people can dictate on how this country is run.

NOW if anybody and I mean anybody who works for any company becomes incompetent in the job they are doing they will fire him immediately NOW WON'T THEY? Now don't you wish that you could have a job where you could get a huge bonus for being totally incompetent. Now you would think that the bank executives who were obviously totally incompetent in allowing the banks to be on the verge of becoming bankrupt would be fired for their incompetence in running and being responsible for the banks becoming bankrupt.

Now instead of firing them they are given millions and millions of dollars in bonuses that end up in totaling 6 or 7 billions of dollars. Now this is total proof that our political system is totally corrupt. Now think about thia. WE have hundreds of other banks in this country that could replace our major banks. NOW DON'T WE? Now being that we live in a global society there are hundreds of foreign banks that would be more than willing to come over here and replace our major bankrupt banks. NOW ISNT THERE?

NOW THINK ABOUT THIS.Ten years or so from now our major banks will again be on the verge of going bankrupt. WHY? BECAUSE I am sure and they are sure that our corrupt politicians will bail them out again. NOW it makes perfect sense for their bank excutives to already be planning on them to become bankrupt again in ten or so years from now. because they are looking forward to get again billions of dollars in bonuses right?

Now this is undisputable proof that our politicians are totally corrupt. Obviously they have proven that they only care about rich people getting richer and poor people getting poorer. NOW DO THEY? Now they state that they can not afford to extend unemployment benefits.or spend 700 billion dollars in a program that would put unemployed people back to work. Now instead we will give 700 billions of dollars to rich people to make them richer and of which we will recieve absolutley no financial benefits from doing so.

Now How Stupid is the government? Well they let all the gas companies raise their gas prices at the same time. If one gas company has a problem producing gas and says it has to raise their price of gas.That is expected. Now What is not acceptable is that all the other gas companies will raise their gas prices to match the price of gas the other company had to raise

Now it is suppose to be illegal to have a monoply in this country. NOW ISN'T IT. But our government lets the gas companies get together and have a monopoly on the price of gas. NOW DON'T THEY?

Now I can remember when gas companies would have gas wars. That was needless to say years ago. Back then gas companies were totaly independent gas companies. They would lower their gas prices to attract new customers.

Now you never hear of any so called independent gas company lowering their price of gas to attract new customers now. Now do you?

Now the gas companies are not stupid they realize and know that there is only X amount of oil left to be pumped out of the ground. And when that is gone they will have no more gas to sell. Now it does not matter if we have enough gas to last lets say twenty or even forty years.

The bottom line is we are going to run out of gas.Now the closer we come to running out of gas the higher the price of gas is going to be. Now the time to make our government do something about it is now. DONT YOU THINK? Now you need to stop and think about this. Do you want to see your children and grand children having to pay twenty dollars for a gallon of gas. And also think about this. The more gas that we use not only in this country but other countries around the world. The quicker we will run out of gas.

NOW REALIZE THIS.Like I stated before we are running out of oil. We no longer are able to produce enough oil to supply our countries needs. Now we have been for years dependent on foreign oil imports. Now when the price of a barrel of foreign oil goes up. It gives our gas companies an excuse to raise the price of gas to any amount they want to.BECAUSE

How to save billions and billions of tax dollars and thousands
and thousands of innocent children, women and men's lives

71

we do not have any way of knowing if they are raising the price of gas accordinaly to the increase in the price of a barrel of oil.

Now also when the price of a barrel of foreign oil is lowered we do not know if the gas companies lower the price of oil accordinaly to the lower price of a barrel of oil. Now what we do know is that our government allows gas companies to make 100 billion dollars a year in profits. because they let gas companies get together and form an illegal monopoly on gas prices.

NOW THINK ABOUT THIS. If gas companies are truly independent. THEN WHY do you not hear of a gas companie advertising on TV that their gas price are lower than other gas companies. ALSO THINK ABOUT THIS WHY don't the so called independent gas companies lower their gas price by lets say just 30 cents or even 20 cents a gallon. BECAUSE if they did that they would be able to make billions and billions of dollars more In profits than the other gas companies. NOW WOULDN'T THEY? NOW ALSO THINK ABOUT THIS. How many companies are able to make 100 billion dollars a year in profits. I can not think of any can you? Now until we can come up with cars that will run on alternate fuel sources. Especially trucks that deliver our consumer goods.

We should insist on our government to impose a 60 percent tax on all profits of over and this is being generous to oil companies 10 billion dollars in profit. NOW DON'T YOU THINK? NOW WAKE UP PEOPLE. The last time the gas companies raised gas prices it hurt our economy big time.One it resulted in higher transportation costs which forced all retail companies to raise their prices on consumer goods like food etc etc. Two IT resulted in people who have to drive to work having less money to buy consumer goods.

Now 70 percent of our economy is based on consumer goods. Now raising gas prices as you now can see has a devastating effect on our economy. Three. IT allowed gas companies to make 100 billion dollars in profit. now our unemployment rate is at an all time high. Now our government says that they are trying to find ways to turn our economy around. RIGHT? Now this is totally ridiculous that our government gives oil companies 8 billion dollars in subsidies.

The poor oil companies say they need it. So they can make 100 billion dollars in profit.NOW PAY ATTENTION. We have the technology to produce cars that will run on renewable fuel sources. We now have electric cars. We have cars that will run on electric and gas. That is a great start. But we need to come out with cars that will run totally on renewable fuel sources. Now I heard on the news that a man developed an alternate renewable fuel source to run his van on. He come up with used vegtable oil and kerosene.

Now this is proof positive that we have the technology to come up with inexpensive alternate fuel sources. To run our cars on. Now it should be absolutely obvious that we have to demand that our government quit giving 8 billion dollars in subsidies to oil companies and use that 8 billion dollars to subsidize companies that will come out with alternate fuel sources to run our cars on.

Now here are some facts that should convince you of the great urgency to demand that our government to subsidize manufactures to come out with cars besides electric that will run on affordable renewable fuel sources. Now as I have previous staded we have the technology to do this. Now we are paying 49 cents more for a gallon of gas then we did a year ago.

Now think about this a year from now we could be paying a $1.00 more for a gallon of gas. NOW COULDN'T WE? They now say that this year mortorist are on track to pay a record 490 billion dollars for gasoline. Now global demand for oil is rising. Now that means one the faster we will run out of oil and two the higher the price of oil will become.

Now at the rate gasoline prices are going up not only will the cost of consumer goods go up and the less money people will have to buy consumers goods but people who work for minimum wages will no longer be able to afford to drive to work. Now you really need to think long and hard about of which I have just stated.

Now after I wrote the above I just found out and this will give you further proof of how corrupt the Republicans and other politicians have become. Now Newt Gringrich Gop's leading candidte in the polls denied that he ever lobbied for Fannie Mae and Fredie Mac,Now over the past decade,Mr Gingrich reportedly got 1.6 million dollars

From the government seized mortgage giants that Mr. Gingrich would tell you contributed mightily to America's decine and its trillion worth of debt. Now that is a great cover up story. DON'T YOU THINK?

Mr Gingrich says the money was for his work as a historian. Now obviously he took the money to influence senior Republicans to be favorable toward Fannie and Freddie.

Mr. Gingrich called his historian work as just another example of his vast experience. NOW PAY ATTENTION FRANNIE AND FREDDIE and out of work people who also have vast experience.I CAN SAVE YOU A TON OF MONEY. INSTEAD of paying Mr Gingrich another 1.6

How to save billions and billions of tax dollars and thousands
and thousands of innocent children, women and men's lives

73

million dollars as a historian. And since Mr Gingrich stated that there is no
lobbying involved in the 1.6 million dollar you paid him to be a historian I
am positive that out of work people with vast experience will work for you
for just 50,000 dollars a year as a historian.

Now you out of work people with vast experience need to start sending
your application to Frannie and Freddie to be a historian. Now Mr Gingrich
and other Republicans state that rich people are job creators. So I am sure
that Frannie and Freddie will hire you out of work people. Right ? Now
I admit I was wrong when I stated that rich people were not job creators.
Obviously they are. They create jobs for politians so they are able to make
millions of dollars. But it is a shame that they don't create jobs for people
who are out of work. Right?

Well I found out that I am not alone on saying that we need to get rid
of corrupt Politicians There is a new book out "THROW THEM ALL
OUT"

It states how Politicians and their friends get rich off of insider stock
tips. Now Mr Gingrich response to the above was I don't think that what is
happening right now is criminal. TRUE BUT IT SHOULD BE RIGHT.

Now what is does prove beyond a shadow of doubt is that our Politicians
are corrupt and huge hypocrites when they state that they are for what is
best for the American people. WHAT a huge joke that has become. Now
think about this. there are 250 millionairs in congress. Now 57 of them
have made it to the ranks of the top 1 percent. Obviously the Republicans
only care about making rich people richer so rich people can make them
richer.

Now we know the real reason why Republicans are HELL bent on
giving rich people tax cuts. because thanks to the rich people they have
become rich people and obviously they dont want to tax themselves. Now
you know why they have no problem in wanting to cut benefits to poor
people and cut Social Security Benefits. It is so they can afford to give rich
people and themselves tax cuts. WE NOW have become economic slaves
to rich people and the Republicans.

WE now have people who have finally woke up to the realization that
rich people and Republicans are in total control on how our government
is run and are out just for themselves. Now they are trying to protest this
by occupying places in our major cities across our country. To demonstrate
against it. Now this has accomplished one thing. It has made people
realize that we have to do something to stop rich people and Republican
from being able to dictate on how this country is run Now I am sorry to

say that they will not accomplish anything by just protesting it. Now if they and you want to make a huge difference on how this country is run SIMPLY put we all have to get together and use our RIGHT TO VOTE IN ORDER to make a huge differance on how our country is run. Now what we have to do and can do is start up a third independent party and vote ALL Republicans out of office.

Now this is just a suggestion but I think that this would be a very appropriate name. THE ROBIN HOOD PARTY. Which will mean that it is a party for the majority of Americans. and that the party's motto is UNITED WE STAND DIVIDED WE FALL. Now I can not emphasize ths enough if you want to have a say in how our government is run. We have to STAND UNITED. Now if we STAND UNITED THIS is just a couple of ways to raise money for the party.

ONE if we have 10 million people donate just ten dollars a piece that will equal 100 million dollars. OR TWO if we have 50 million people donate just two dollars a piece that will equal 100 million dollars as you can see we will be able to raise any amount of money we want to if WE STAND UNITED. NEEDLESS to say rich people wont be able to raise that amount of money for the Republican party or any other party. NOW WILL THEY?

NOW we live in an age of instant communiction. Now it will be simple and easy with our computers and cell phones to spread the word about our NEW PARTY NOW WON'T IT? The Bottom line is that you have the power to decide on how this country is run. NOW WAKE UP. You have to take away the power to run this country from the Republicans and rich people. YOU also have to realize this. Republicans and rich people do not care if you are employed or not. Homeless or not or starving or not.

They only care about making themselves richer. NOW the choice is entirely up to you to make. You Have to Decide if you want to be employed,have a home, or be able to feed yourself and family OR NOT. Now this is just a couple of more signs that need to know of what the Republicans are up to.

The Republicans now obviously believe that there is absolutely nothing wrong with our economy and that there are plenty of jobs available for people to get. WHY else would the Republicans who are trying to win the primarys for president.Make statements like this. People who occupy wall street and other places in this country should quit protesting and go out and get a job.

And people who no longer are able to afford to feed themselves or their family and are starving should just go out and get a job. BECAUSE they belive that there are plenty of jobs available to you to have that you will be able to not only feed. Yourself but if you have a family your family too. And also be able to provide yourself and family with a roof over your head. Now if you lose your job and become unemployed and can no longer provide for yourself and family is not because you can not find another job is is because you are too damn lazy to go out and find one of the plentiful jobs that they say are available to support yourself and your family. You have to understands that the Republicans know why you dont have a job to support yourself or your family. it is not because they believe that there are no jobs available it is because they believe that you are too damn lazy to go out and get a job.

Now they also believe that they need to do whatever it takes to help get 12 more Republican sentors elected. BECAUSE this will give them complete and total controll on how this country is run and you will no longer have absolutely no say so on how this country is run.

CHAPTER 9

NOW I was in the process of going over this book and sending it off to be published. UNTIL I heard what the Republican Party is up to. NOW This is a Chapter that I have to add to this book. NOW this should be a HUGE WAKE UP CALL and I do mean a Huge WAKE UP CALL to poor hard working Americans. NOW as the old saying went. THE hand writing is on the wall and WAKE UP and smell the roses.

NOW the following are undisputable SIGNS AND FACTS that the Republican Party has become an AMERICAN NAZI PARTY. The Republican Party believes in NAZIFICATION which means in having complete and total control in how a government is run

NOW pay attention. First you need a little history lesson. THE German People voted for the NAZI Party in 1933. NOW when the NAZI Party took over the GERMAN Government they had complete and total dictorial power on how the German People lived from 1933 to 1945. Now the first thing they did was take away the German Peoples right to vote

NOW the dictionary describes a NAZI as being a HARSHLY DOMINEERING AND DICTORIAL PERSON. THAT describes the Republican Party to a T. There is no better way to describe the Repuplian Party than that. NOW IS THERE. NOW you have to WAKE UP AND REALIZE THIS. Now the following are facts to prove that the Republicans are a NAZI Party.

Now under President BUSH the Republicans raised our national debt seven times. Now under our Democratic President the Republians refused to raise our national debt knowing that if we did not raise it. It would totally devastate our economy if their demands were NOT met. The Democrates had absolutely no choice but to give in to their demands. One of which was not to raise taxes on rich people. Which proves that Republicans only care about rich people and do not give a damn about poor hard working Americans. NOW DO THEY?

Now that is not what you can call democrocy at work. That is what you call Nazism at work. NOW ISNT IT? Now after the Republicans did that They destabilized our stock market it now goes up and down like a yo yo. They also caused our triple A credit rating to drop to A double A credit rating. Now everybody shout out HAIL Republicans. Now terrorist groups could not have done a better job of trying to destroy our economy. NOW COULD THEY?

Now before our national debt became an issue. The Republicans voted over whelmingly to raise our national debt by 15 billion dollars by increasing our national defense budget. Now how did they say that they were going to pay for this increase. IT sure was not to raise taxes on rich people but to cut benifits on food stamps to poor people. AGAIN HAIL REPUBLICANS. Now again the NAZI PARTY took away the German peoples right to vote.

NOW this is what the Republican Party is trying to do. NOW Pay attention 8 or 9 Republican Governors got together and decided to and did dictate to the people of their states that they would be required to have a government photo ID to be eligible to vote. NOW the point is this not that they decided to have people have a goverment photo I.D in order to vote of which they did not need to do but that they dictated that you need a governnment photo I.D in order to vote.

NOW if they would have put this proposal before the people that lived in their states and the people would have voted to approve of this proposal. That would have been democracy at work. NOW since they dictated this proposal that is what you call NAZISM at work. NOW it dosn't stop there. NOW the Republicans want to propose and dictate that only property owners will have a right to vote, YOU heard right that only property owners will have the right to vote. THINK ABOUT THAT. That also will mean that veterans who do not own property will be denied the right to vote. THINK ABOUT THAT.

Now as you can see the Republicans are and will keep trying to come up with ways to take our right to vote away. Now the Republicans have six ways to lower our National debt. ONE They already did this they increased our national defense spending by 15 billion dollars. TWO They want to continue to give tax breaks to the rich. THREE They want to give corporations huge tax breaks. FOUR They want to cut back on giving food stamps to the poor. FIVE they want to do away with medicare. SIX They want to do away with Social Security Benefits.

NOW you Republicans are TOTAL AND COMPLETE IDIOTS. ONE HOW do you plan on taking care of the millions of poor people and senior citizen If you take away their benefits ? I can only assume that you will sit back and watch them starve to death or build gas chambers and give them a choice STARVE TO DEATH OR BE GASED TO DEATH. NOW if that is not your plan what the hell is your plan to take care of them.Now pay Attention 70% of our economy is based on consumer goods.

Now what the hell good is it going to do to give tax breaks to rich people and corporations. Do you think that they will go out buy more consumer goods with it idiots? They already have all the consumer goods they need like A house,cars etc. Now how brilliant is your idea to cut benefits to poor people and senior citizen? THAT means that millions and millions of people will not be able to afford to buy food and consumer goods. NOW WILL THEY?

THAT will mean that our economy will be totally destroyed. Now rich people and corporations will end up losing billion of dollars because millions and millions of people will no longer be able to afford to buy their product or services. NOW WILL THEY IDIOTS? NOW WAKE UP. They now say that we should cut back on medicare benefits. IF they do that it will mean that people on Social Security will have less money to spend on consumer goods, IDIOTS.

Now pay attention rich people NOW IF The Republicans take controll of our government and deny millions of people right to vote OF which they are in the process of trying to do. THEY will no longer need your millions of dollars to get elected. NOW WILL THEY? They will then be able to turn the tables on you. If you don't do what they tell you to do. They will simply threaten to raise your taxes big time.

NOW if you still want to vote for Republicans AFTER you vote for them. You make sure to raise your right hand into the air and shout out HAIL Republicans HAIL Republicans. Because that will more than likely be the last time you will have the right to vote.Now what are you rich people planning on doing with the money that you get from the tax breaks that you get.

It sure as hell isnt going to create jobs. THAT IS FOR SURE. The only thing that I can think of is that you believe that you can take it with you to your grave and spend it in your after life. Now if you were smart you would want to pay your fair share of taxes. Because simply put it would greatly help turn our economy around. WHICH you would then be able to make more millions of dollars that you now get by having tax breaks and that will allow you to take more money to your graves and spend it in your after life. DONT YOU THINK?

Now here are some hard fact that you have to realize. The U.S. Census Bureau stated that U.S. median house hold income slipped 2,3% in 2010 to 49,445 dollars.meadian means half make less than that and that means a family of four are making less than 22,314 dollars. The poor grew to 46.2 million people in 2010. From 43.6 million in 2009 yielding a 15.1 percent proverty rate.

The census data show its the fourth consecutive annual rise in the poverty rate. Now over the last 6 years Republicans have been giving tax breaks to rich people. They say giving tax breaks to rich people creates jobs. Now I have just stated that our poor population has grown based on cold hard facts. I will ask and you should too. Ask the Republicans to come up with cold hard facts to state how many jobs rich people have created with their tax breaks.

Think long and hard about this fact. They state that rich people make up less than 2 percent of our population. Now it should be obvious that we have to vote Republicans out of office. UNLESS you want to continue to let less than two percent of our population and Republicans dictate on how our country is run. Now as I have stated before we have to start up a third party that will represent the majority of the American people. UNLESS you dont want to have a say in how our country is run. Now I have stated this before. BUT I can not over emphasize this enough. NOW 70 percent of our economy is based on consumer goods. WHICH means the more people are able to spend on consumer goods the stronger our economy will be.

Now if we increase Social Security payments by 800 dollars a month. This will have huge economic impact. Unlike giving rich people tax breaks which has absolutely no economic impact. People on Social Security will spend that money on consumer goods. NOW WON'T THEY?

Now it will put millions of people back to work and decrease our poor population. Now here is how we pay for this increase in Social Security Benefits. ONE We have to reduce our national defense spending by 200 billion dollars a year. Now over A five year period that will mean A trillion dollars saved. That will still leave 500 billion dollars A year of which means that over A 5 year period two and a half trillion dollars will be spend on national defense. Now since we are now living in A Global Society that is still way too much money to spend on national defense. NOW DON'T YOU THINK?

TWO Have rich people and corporations pay their fair share of taxes. Which will result in billions and billions of dollars in yearly revenue. THREE Legalize drugs and prostitution. That will save billion and billions of dollars every year.FOUR Ban firearms. That will save billion and billions of dollars every year. FIVE The millions of people we put back to work will be paying billions and billion of dollars into federal taxes and into Social Security. Now that is how we can pay for the increase and continue to be able to pay for it.

NOW I have stated at the begining of this book THE majority of people in the country is made up of IDIOTS AND HYPOCRITES. Now don't you think that it is time that you stop being IDIOTS AND HYPROCRITES? NOW PAY ATTENTION. You have the power to vote for Politiicans that will make the above changes that will turn our economy completely around and create jobs, and make this a safer country to live in for yourself,children,and grand children by banning fire arms.

THE BOTTOM LINE Is is this you the voters of this country have the power to dictate on how this country is run. UNLESS you want to continue to let rich people and Republicans dictate on how this country is run. THIE CHOICE IS YOURS TO MAKE.

Chapter 10

NOW A SUMMATION. Now don't you think that we need to elect politicians who will vote for what is best for our American society as a whole and not for their own political agendas. We can save billions and billions of dollars by legalizing drugs and prostitution. We can put drug cartels and drug dealers out of business. We can stop teenagers from having any access to drugs.

Now we can save billions and billions of dollars by putting a limit on how much we spend on national defense. Now by banning firearms we can save billions and billions of dollars that we now spend on prosecuting people and keeping them in jail for long periods of time for illegal use of firearms. And we can also prevent and stop stupid idiots from being able to go out and buy firearms and kill as many innocent children,woman and men as they want to.

Now when you lose your job or are now jobless and lose your home and are homeless. Also when you lose a loved one like a spouse, a young son or daughter, or a good friend because somebody shot them to death. You will have nobody to blame but yourself. Now you have a huge choice to make. You can make this a safer country to live in or not. Also a prosperous country to live in or not. Again the choice is yours to make.

NOW WORLD YOU HAVE TO WAKE UP. You have to forget trying to live in the past. The past is now history and we can not change it. We can learn from it and change the way we now live for the betterment of humanity. Our human race is now living in a global society run by a global economy. Now realize this. We all are now nothing more or less than human beings sharing this planet. Earth that we live on needless to say we all have to learn to take care of it because this is the only planet we have to live on.

Now as I have stated in this country we have to ban the sale and manufacturing of firearms to save lives and make this a safer country to live in. Now to all countries of the world. You also have to ban the sale and manufacturing of firearms to save lives and make this a safer world to live in. Now look at this economically. This is the u;timate in stupidity. To sit back and watch your customers being shot to death because you have the ability to prevent them from doing this by banning firearms.

Now understand this the easiest way to kill a person is with a gun. So don't you think we should make it as difficult as possible to kill off your customers.NOW DON'T YOU THINK? Now there is one more thing that not only in this country but all countries of the world HAVE TO DO AND I MEAN HAVE TO DO. Now no matter what your political religious or any other views that you have we can all agree on this. THAT HUMAN LIFE HAS TO BE REGARDED AS BEING SACRED. That it is totally unacceptable to kill or harm a fellow human being. The way that we can help to insure that we accomplish this is to educate all children of the world from pre school and every year until they graduate and beyond that human life is scared. That it is totally unaceptable and wrong to kill or cause any physical harm to a fellow human being.

The fate of our human race depends on this. Because we are not the only inteligent race of beings who live in this universe. Now this universe that we live in is so vast that we really do not know how vast it is. Now you have to be a complete and TOTAL IDIOT to believe that we are totally the only intelligent beings in this vast universe. Now do you really believe that God would create a vast universe for us alone to live in.NO HE WOULD NOT Now we have the means with our nuclear weaponss to destroy all life on this planet. It has only been by the grace of God that we have not wiped ourselfs off the face of this planet. If we would do that then God would have nobody left on this planet to worship him. NOW WOULD HE? Now you can state we have no proof that intelligent life exsits on other planets in our universe but obviously there is

NOW PAY ATTENTION Here is a little history lesson of the human race. Now before Columbus discovered America in 1492. The civilized countries of that time period had absolutely no way of knowing or had any written proof like being stated in the bible that the continents of North and South America even existed with intelligent life at that time. Now what did the civilized countries at that time do when they found out that the continets of North and South America existed with intelligent human beings.

Now the civilized countries for their own selfish reasons went there and slaughtered the intelligent inhabitants and took over their countries. Now since then we have had many wars and two World Wars. Now we as a human race have proven to aliens beyond a shadow of doubt that for our selfish reasons we have absolutely no regards for or respect for human life. THEREFORE They know that we would have absolutely no regard for or respect for any alien life forms that we would encounter NOW WOULD WE?

Now aliens have been observing us for years and years. Now if they wanted to they could have and are able to wipe us off the face of this earth anytime that they want to. Now the reason that they don't and will not make contact with us. IS THAT THEY ARE NOT IDIOTS. LIKE WE ARE. Now aliens do not judge us by the color of our skin, our political views or our religious views. The judge us solely as a murderous human race that has absolutely no respect for human or alien life forms. The bottom line is this. as long as we have no respect for human life we will never have any respect for alien life.

They know that if they try to land on earth in their space ship that we would shoot them to death in a heartbeat. Let's say that they would be ten feet tall and green. We would say that they are monsters from outer space and shoot and kill them. Now even if they looked like us. We would still consider them as monsters from outer space and shoot and kill them. Now wouldnt we? I know that if I was an alien that I would not risk my life to try and make contact with a murderous human race. NOW WOULD YOU.

Now the movie AVATAR is a perfect and I do mean perfect example of how we would treat alien life forms that we would encounter by traveling to the stars. We would slaughter them without even blinking an eye and try to wipe them all out. Now over the last 50 years we have made great strides in our technological advancement. So it is very conceivable that in the next 50 to 200 years that we could develope the ability to travel to the stars.

Now unless we can learn to hold human life as being sacred before that day comes. The day that we do develope the ability to travel to the stars will be our day of armageddon. Now aliens will have no choice but to come here and wipe us off the face of this planet earth. Because we have a long history of killing innocent human beings on this planet. They know that we would not even think twice about killing innocent alien beings for our own selfish reasons.

Now simply put if we can learn to hold human life as being sacred we will have two benefits of this One aliens will not come and wipe us off the face of this planet earth. Two aliens will be able to make contact with us without having to worry about being killed. Now the benefits of us making contact with aliens will be pun intended astronomical. The bottom line is this It is not up to the aliens whether we live or die as a human race. THE CHOICE IS OURS ALONE TO MAKE.